UNCONVENTIONAL

JAMIE ANDREA GARZOT

UNCONVENTIONAL

A MEMOIR OF
ENTREPRENEURISM,
POLITICS, AND
POT

GIRL FRIDAY BOOKS

*The conversations and events described in this book are based on the
author's memories. Others may remember these events differently.
Some names have been changed to preserve the anonymity of others.*

GFB GIRL FRIDAY BOOKS

Published by Girl Friday Books™, Seattle
www.girlfridaybooks.com

Produced by Girl Friday Productions

Design: Paul Barrett
Production editorial: Bethany Davis
Project management: Katherine Richards

Image credits: cover image © Reinhardt Kenneth

ISBN (hardcover): 978-1-954854-29-1
ISBN (e-book): 978-1-954854-40-6

Library of Congress Control Number: 2021920317

First edition

*To Andrew, for planting the seed that finally took root;
and to Jim, for insisting that I cultivate it.*

CONTENTS

Foreword by Lori Ajax ix

Introduction xi

That Road 1
Insomnia 3
The Vision 10
The Green Lights 15
Finding My Voice 19
Legal Cannabis 101 26
The Accidental Expert 31
The Wild West 37
The Cops 46
The Motherless Daughter 50
The Husband 58
Edibles and Algebra 67
Small-Town Politics 76
The Three Little Piggies . . . and the Big Bad Wolf 81
Church, Jameson, and Laughter 88
The Capitol 91
The IRS 101
That Assemblymember 107
Crazy Is as Crazy Does 111
Synergy 119
Outreach, Sexual Reproduction, and Lube 128

The Cash 136
The Team 146
Greed 158
Epilogue 166

Afterword by Jim Wood 171

Acknowledgments 175

About the Author 179

FOREWORD

Looking back, writing a foreword to a book on the cannabis industry was never part of the plan . . . definitely not. In fact, working with the cannabis industry was not something I ever expected to happen in my life.

My cannabis journey started five years ago and changed my life forever. I would like to think fate intervened, because I was an unlikely candidate. I was virtually unknown to the cannabis industry; I never smoked or consumed cannabis, and here I was being tapped by the Governor's Office to head up the Bureau of Cannabis Control, an agency that hadn't even been created yet but was expected to regulate this newly legalized California cannabis industry.

The mere thought of undertaking this tremendous task was both intimidating and terrifying. I kept telling myself this was not for me, but my gut was tugging at me to accept this appointment. It was a challenge of a lifetime and a chance to quell those feelings in my heart that I was not good enough.

It was a grueling task that tested every facet of my being, including learning from the ground up about this remarkable and resilient industry. It was leadership boot camp even for the most seasoned regulator. Along the way, I encountered extreme highs and lows, lots of self-reflection, anxiety, teamwork, and personal sacrifices, and I finally learned to accept the accomplishments despite the criticisms.

I will always be grateful for the opportunity to serve the cannabis industry and all the wonderful people I met along the way. Jamie was someone I came to know and respect during this journey. Strong and fiercely independent, she is a passionate force who always gave her opinion even when I did not necessarily want to hear it! She was committed to the cause of making cannabis legalization work.

Jamie's unique personal story takes you through the tumultuous legalization of the biggest cannabis market in the nation. It is raw, honest, and unexpected . . . not unlike Jamie.

Lori Ajax
Chief, Bureau of Cannabis Control (2016–2020)
California's first "Cannabis Czar"

INTRODUCTION

A $5,000 stack of one-hundred-dollar bills has a volume of approximately sixteen cubic inches. This means that $100,000 can fit comfortably in an average shoebox. In turn, the cargo compartment of my SUV can hold two such shoeboxes next to the spare tire. It is ludicrous that I should have cause to know the above data points, but they are part of the reality that goes with running an all-cash cannabis business that cannot access the banking system due to its conflict with federal law.

When driving the two hundred miles from Redding back to my home in Santa Rosa at the end of the workweek, or simply driving from one of the stores across town, in my shiny black SUV, obeying all traffic laws while SiriusXM Chill plays softly through the Harman/Kardon speakers, I am just another vehicle on the road. Except for my personal protection K9, Zeus, riding in the back seat. And those two shoeboxes.

That I was comfortable with the "uncomfortability" of carrying $200,000, give or take, in the cargo compartment of my vehicle on any given day of the week is not in any way, shape, or form normal. While this may certainly have been an unconventional way to diversify my assets, it was also insane, preposterous, and completely unsafe.

Ironically, my entering the cannabis industry was never about the money. Most people will not believe me when I say that I didn't get into this industry to become rich. That is the stereotype, but those who know me well understand that I have never been motivated by money.

So, if not for the money, then why did I do it?

Why did I exchange my well-paying corporate job for the risk of starting such a highly controversial small business in a staunchly conservative part of Northern California?

Why did I make the decision to open a cannabis store seven years before full legalization, during a time in which the industry was truly another Wild West?

To see if I could.

And while that is definitely part of the answer, it is also a gross oversimplification.

The unconventional spirit that has been at my core for as long as I can remember was in the driver's seat again, and I knew it would be one hell of a ride. Even the fact that I wanted to run my own business defied convention, given that my degree is in English, not business. I'm a word nerd, not a number cruncher, for f's sake.

In fact, "unconventional" is quite possibly the single best word that describes not only who I am but also the way in which I have pursued my vision, built my businesses, and ultimately how I have sculpted my life, before, during, and beyond cannabis.

Starting with the launch of my first store in 2009, even knowing that I was starting down a path that was sure to be fraught with challenges, I never could have imagined the fantastic journey that was to follow.

This is the story of that journey; a journey of the incidents that molded me, the laws that guided me, the people who helped and inspired me. It is also the story of the principles that I learned, honed, and refined over the course of my journey as an unlikely entrepreneur in an industry that was taking shape on the fly.

But, above all else, this is a story about never—even in the face of overwhelming, oftentimes seemingly insurmountable odds—giving up on yourself or your vision.

Come with me and experience this incredible cannabis adventure—one that, like any journey, began with a road . . .

THAT ROAD

The Robert Frost poem is timeless for good reason: its simple beauty has touched and inspired millions, myself included.

It'd be great to say that I read Frost's words at a young age and was so moved that I subsequently decided to always take the path less traveled. But that would be to credit me with foresight I didn't have. In retrospect, however, that road less traveled has presented itself to me time and again, and it has been the one that I have chosen often, sometimes consciously, sometimes not.

The times I have consciously chosen that road have often been the result of envisioning what ninety-year-old me would want present-day me to do.

I also saw the concept of the well-traveled road as a safety net. I mean, if I got down the less traveled one and walked into a shit tornado, I could always backtrack, right?

But it is often a risk, that road less traveled—a big one—and one not many people can understand taking.

I remember telling my dad (who had been christened "Dean" but dubbed "Jocko," a childhood nickname that he carried his whole life) about my decision to open a medical cannabis store, a decision that meant, of course, that I had to leave my corporate job at Pacific Gas & Electric Company.

We were talking over the phone, and I could visualize him scratching his head, literally and figuratively, when he asked me why I would leave such a secure position with an excellent company to go out and start my own business—and a "pot shop," of all things. He was incredulous.

I told him this was something I had to do; I had to try. He should have remembered that I always thrive on a challenge.

I also told him that if I failed, there would be time enough for me to go back to the well-traveled road and find another job. There would always be another job if I needed one, whereas there might not ever be another opportunity like the one before me; I meant to seize it.

While my motivation was idealistic and my family circle had always encouraged the concept of following one's dream, I was pushing the envelope this time.

Perhaps this is why I never gave up, even during the most difficult, harrowing hours of my journey. But I know it's also because I am quite stubborn and have always been fiercely competitive, always driven to succeed and to win.

This was one of the times I consciously took the road less traveled, and it indeed made all the difference.

INSOMNIA

The clock on my nightstand glowed cheerily in the darkness, proudly displaying the time as 3:00 a.m. Giving it a dirty look, I rolled over, plumped up my pillow for what felt like the hundredth time, and tried not to think about how tired I was going to be the next day. Where was this insomnia coming from? Morpheus had always been a dear and intimate friend, but out of nowhere he'd ditched me, abandoning me to the mercies of that damn clock.

After struggling through a couple of weeks of that insomnia bullshit, I decided enough was enough, but it wasn't cannabis I reached for. While it seems ironic now, I didn't initially think about cannabis as a remedy for insomnia, and with good reason: I was not a pot smoker. I'm still not.

"How in the world did you get into this industry?" is the one question I know, without fail, I'm going to be asked anytime I speak or present on cannabis. This is the unabridged version of my answer that I have given countless times.

I am not of "cannabis heritage" (a term used within the industry, particularly with regard to growers), meaning I didn't grow up around it; I didn't have parents who used or grew cannabis. I never even smoked it in high school. My dad was emphatic about a couple of things. He told me not to use drugs and not to get pregnant while living under his roof. Good news—I succeeded on both counts! I have managed to dodge the pregnancy bullet my entire life, and my first experience with cannabis didn't come until I smoked a joint in my college dorm room as a freshman. So cliché.

I remember thinking as I watched my new college friend pull a plastic baggie from her jacket and very ceremoniously lay it on the table that I was doing something *really* bad. The subsequent thought after my girlfriend and I had smoked that joint was to wonder what the hell the big deal was. The high wasn't that appealing, and I had never been a smoker of any-thing. I didn't feel the need to repeat the experience anytime soon.

I was and have continued to be completely ambivalent about the effect of cannabis recreationally. I find it "meh." If I want a head change, I prefer a beer or whiskey. Even during my eleven years saturated in the industry, surrounded by endless product samples, I never became a recreational cannabis user.

In fact, my lack of recreational interest and subsequently low tolerance were legendary amongst my staff and a constant source of amusement for them. Several of my more-veteran team members loved to tell newbies the story about the time I inadvertently consumed cannabis-infused edibles in the mid-dle of a workday.

It was company policy that the chef for the in-house edibles line, 530 Edibles, always make non-infused prototypes of any new products she wanted to bring online so that I could give my final stamp of approval before they hit the shelf. One after-noon, the chef made a scrumptious pumpkin concoction—fabulous treats—of which I enthusiastically approved. The following day, having skipped lunch, I found my mouth starting to water when I spied a small plastic container of the delicacies in the kitchen refrigerator. The container wasn't marked "infused," so I assumed they weren't. We all know the saying about assumption being the mother of all fuckups.

When the chef came back into the kitchen and saw that I was well into polishing off the contents of that container, the look on her face told me all I needed to know. To this day, I don't think my staff has ever seen me pack up my laptop, throw the dogs in the car, and get the hell out of there as fast as I did that afternoon.

I managed to get safely home and on my couch before the effects hit and the drooling started. I have no problem being the butt of my own joke, and this one made for a popular story in the years to come. And the chef never again forgot to label a container as "infused."

But I digress.

After that one joint at college, it would be years before I would again try cannabis. Throughout my early adulthood, I had only fleeting relationships—one-night stands—with the drug. If it was at a party and offered, I might partake, but I never sought it out, never purchased it for myself.

It wasn't until I was into my thirties that cannabis factored into my life in any significant way. I think I voted for Proposition 215, California's medical cannabis ballot initiative, in 1996, but I can't be sure. I'm not even sure that I voted that year, I'm now embarrassed to say.

However, in 2008, for whatever reason, my brain started to come awake at 2:00 or 3:00 a.m., disrupting the beautiful sleep I had enjoyed every night of my life up until that point.

I tried a couple of over-the-counter sleep aids, but I didn't like the way they made me feel the next day. I went to the doctor and tried prescription sleep aids with the same result. Then a friend asked me if I had tried cannabis. I said I had but that

I didn't really like smoking it, and I didn't care for the high all that much. They explained that cannabis edibles worked great to combat insomnia, and, given that I would've tried anything at this point, I experimented with some.

I was amazed at how soundly I slept and, more important, how refreshed I felt in the morning. I woke clear-headed and energized for the day. Quite literally overnight, I became a believer and went out and got my medical cannabis recommendation.

With the doctor's medical cannabis note hot in my hands, I started looking for cannabis stores in which to shop. While in San Francisco for a weekend, I sought out a couple of the available storefronts. A few weekends later, I was in Sacramento and checked out several more. There was even one open in Redding, my locale at that time, so I stopped in.

What I found was that in every single case, the stores were all similar and, most important, they all focused on the "420 lifestyle" (a lifestyle encompassing regular cannabis use), something with which I did not identify and to which I couldn't relate.

In 2008, I was working as a community relations rep for Pacific Gas &Electric, and, as a thirtysomething business professional, I was looking for a medical-cannabis shopping experience with which I could identify and feel at ease. But it didn't seem to exist.

I saw the potential to create a store that was different, that did not have the "stoner" customer at its center but instead embraced *all* customers. I envisioned a store and an environment inclusive to everyone, regardless of their cannabis background and experience; a store in which everyone, be they a lifelong consumer or a business professional using cannabis for occasional insomnia, could feel comfortable.

The common denominator in any job I'd had since entering the workforce at fifteen and a half years old was customer service; it was in my blood, and it was the obvious and natural decision for me to make the customer the focus of my prospective operation as opposed to the product. Specifically, I wanted more engagement with the customer, especially with regard to their level of experience with cannabis. Being a newcomer myself to its medical usage, I didn't want to assume that every customer who walked into the store knew exactly what they wanted or even that they were comfortable being there. This meant getting to know the customer, asking open-ended questions, and having them rank their prior cannabis usage on a scale from one to ten. Customer service meant making each person who walked into the store feel special. It meant listening to them.

It was on this premise that I based the foundation for 530 Collective (the term "collective" always felt awkward to me, but that was the term the state wanted used), but I had to fight for it. "John," my husband at the time, was still working his job while I was managing the entire 530 Collective operation. However, he had 50 percent interest in the endeavor, and he didn't like my idea. He said it would never work because it was too different from what everyone else was doing. The importance of making the business stand out was my point precisely, and, fueled even further by his challenge, I was adamant about my concept. Several arguments ensued, but we reached a compromise. Since John was the cannabis connoisseur, he would have carte blanche when it came to the products we carried and the plants. Because my forte was sales and customer service, I handled absolutely everything else operationally, from policies and procedures to internal forms and bookkeeping, from logo and interior design to customer experience and staff training, right down to every single component of outreach.

The ambience that I envisioned for 530 was also critically different from what I had experienced as a client. As a business owner, you have the incredible opportunity to set the stage for the entire customer experience from the second they walk through your door by the ambience—the vibe—that you create. All of the stores I had visited in 2008 and 2009 felt a lot like head shops. They were seedy, their dimly lit lobbies often decorated with black lights and glowing wall decor, their dispensing rooms offering a clandestine, living-room drug-deal vibe.

I remember walking into a dispensing room and being helped by a kid wearing baggy jeans, his shaggy hair mostly covered by a low-slung hat, under the brim of which I could just make out his glassy eyes. His less-than-professional garb contrasted so sharply with the business-casual attire I happened to be wearing that day that I felt completely out of place.

He greeted me with a chin-nod and a "Whassup." I chin-nodded back in response and looked behind him to the shelves holding the big jars of cannabis flower. Each jar, labeled with the strain it contained, was accompanied by what looked like a hand-drawn graphic novel illustration—quite well done, actually—many of which, inexplicably, featured incredibly well-endowed women. Now, for the record, I'm no prude and I have nothing against boobs, having two of them myself. They're lovely, and I quite like them. But there's a time and a place, and smack on the front of medicinal-product packaging in a business purporting to be legitimate was neither.

Two jars in particular caught my attention, but for a different reason: I was drawn by the strain names represented on their front. "Cat Piss," read one, accompanied by a Halloween-cat-type graphic. Was that name supposed to make me want it? The other jar was labeled "Fire Crotch." Fire Crotch??? You've got to be fucking kidding me. I fortunately cannot remember what graphic accompanied that one. I left that store, knowing I could build out an establishment more welcoming than a "Fire Crotch" vibe, and I knew I could give better customer service than a "Whassup."

In making the customer the focal point, the driving force of the business then becomes the customer experience. The product itself is obviously necessary, but in my model, it took a back seat to creating an experience that focused on professionalism, ambience, and knowledge first with the commodity itself second.

In the end, 530 Collective emerged onto the market as something new and different, just as I had wanted. This was my formula from the very beginning. It was an unconventional formula to which I held and continued to fine-tune over the years. It is this simple formula—a nuanced yet intentional shift from the head-shop vibe the industry embraced in 2009 to the clean, professional, upscale establishment I envisioned—to which I attribute both the early as well as the sustained success of my stores.

THE VISION

My job as a community relations rep with PG&E was fun, dynamic, and interesting. But the idea of opening a different type of cannabis store had begun sneaking into my workdays. Whether I was seated at my desk or out in the field conducting an energy audit, the idea persisted to the point of becoming almost an obsession. The more I thought about it, the more vivid the vision became: a store centrally located in a good part of town, not in some dingy alley; a bright, modern, and welcoming storefront with relaxing music softly playing; a store into which anyone could walk and feel comfortable; a store providing an experience that made each customer feel special.

The next most frequent question I am asked is, How do I do it? The *it* being subjective, of course. *It* might be achieving success in general, or the behind-the-scenes work of the operation, or the never-ending advocacy work, or staying the course in the face of any adversity. In fact, *it* is all of those things.

Whatever your personal *it* is, the starting point is always the same: a clear vision. It can be something small and simple to begin with. In fact, it should be. It will come into more detailed focus with time and attention.

It's easy to see the end result, the physical manifestations of success in the form of a popular product, a busy store, the passage of cannabis law reform, or a healthy bank account. However, it is not always easy to see how any of those successes began, where they started, or what that initial first step was that led down the path of success. Yet, all successes start the same way, with a vision. Somewhat paradoxically, the vision is both the beginning and the end.

There are countless books on the law of attraction, manifesting your desires, creative visualization, and the like. In no way can I claim to be a teacher of the subject while I continue to be a student. My classroom has been my life experiences, and I can share only those, along with my perspective on how holding tightly to a vision is paramount to any success.

Having always been an avid reader, and not knowing exactly what I wanted to be when I grew up, I chose a major that I knew would interest me: literature. Upon graduation, I was, perhaps surprisingly, offered a job in Old Navy's management-training program in their Mission Valley store in San Diego. Despite my lack of any business background, I accepted because the job aligned with a lot of my prior work experience in customer service. It was during my stint with Old Navy that the desire to one day own my own business began to develop, and over the next decade, I would toy with different sparks of ideas: a coffeehouse (in the pre-Starbucks era), a surf shop completely geared toward women, a ladies' clothing store. None of these ideas ever developed beyond sparks in my mind, but from the very beginning, retail was the commonality with all of them. And the desire to one day make my dream a reality smoldered.

After I became a medical cannabis patient in 2008 and experienced dissatisfaction with the stores available at that time, it was logical that those sparks would rekindle, allowing me to see the retail cannabis opportunity clearly, and that my subsequent vision would begin to form. Yet never having taken a business course, I went into this venture in almost every way cold, without a scrap of business know-how, without a road map, and with no experience. I didn't know what I didn't know. All I had was my dream, and again—my vision. I knew what I wanted to see as the end result. While I didn't realize it at the time, this was probably a huge advantage. My business naivete left me unburdened as to the challenges and pitfalls of business ownership. I would face those challenges and pitfalls in due time, but their absence in the beginning gave me more freedom, freedom to simply create; to give my vision full rein without doubt and fear poking their heads in, disrupting my focus.

As the idea of opening a medical cannabis collective began to take root in 2008 and into 2009, there were any number of legitimate obstacles that could have proven insurmountable should I have chosen to examine them.

And looking back at the laundry list of odds against me, it's probably a good thing I never examined them in detail. But, at the time, I never considered or focused on any of the many reasons why I might fail or the many reasons I might not have been able to bring my vision to life. I suppose that subconsciously I knew that giving any amount of attention to the obstacles ahead or to failure would crack the door for doubt to enter, and once allowed in, the parade of "what if" questions that would inevitably follow could be fatal. I simply left that door firmly closed and instead focused on what I wanted to see as an end result.

But let's take a look at that list now, just for fun:

• It was a "pot shop."
• I didn't have an effing clue how to run a business.
• I had never done anything remotely like this before (I don't think my lemonade stand in the driveway when I was eight exactly counts).

- I had only a four-figure capital investment to get the business off the ground.
- I wasn't sure I could find a landlord willing to rent a building to a cannabis-business owner.
- I did not have any cash reserves.
- The city could have decided not to let me open a store.
- Cannabis was still socially taboo to a certain extent, even in progressive California.
- While the Obama administration was supposed to be friendly to the industry, there weren't many stores in existence.
- California's fledgling industry was completely unregulated by the state and still very much a "Wild West."
- Other than what I was using to help me sleep, I wasn't a heavy cannabis user, and customers might expect me to have more personal experience with the product than I actually did.
- The federal government could intervene and show up on my retail doorstep anytime with guns drawn.

Not being utterly naive, I knew full well that failure was always an option. But I knew it in a theoretical way, not in an emotional way, and it is emotions that fuel vision.

For many, that may not seem like a good enough reason to take such a risk. After all, I was walking away from an excellent job—a job I enjoyed—with an outstanding company to venture into the great unknown. But walk away I did, and I never looked back.

While I don't think that my actions were understood, I will say that no one in my life was in direct opposition, which was helpful. Even had I been faced with direct opposition, I know I still would have pursued my dream, but with no direct opposition, there was one fewer bullet on my list.

Having support from those closest to you can be helpful. However, you must not let your vision live or die by their sword. Your belief in the validity of your vision and your faith and confidence in your own ability to bring it to life are what matter; those two components must always be paramount in your mind, held in sharp focus beyond any obstacles.

Writing these words now, it seems so easy. It is and yet it isn't.

THE GREEN LIGHTS

Kristine Brooks had no good reason to rent me her building and a lot of solid reasons not to. Located in the central part of the City of Shasta Lake and situated on a corner of the main drag, Kristine's building was one of the nicest in town with an attractive brick exterior, loads of plate glass windows, and jasmine flowers creeping along the brick.

Although the building was vacant, there was no "For Lease" sign in the window, as my several drive-bys confirmed. I had even pulled into the parking lot and peeked in the windows on a couple of occasions, looking for any clue as to who owned it, but without luck. Every time I drove by, I fell more in love with the building. The interior was already laid out ideally with a check-in counter and seating area. I could see myself behind the counter, welcoming customers and chatting with them while I verified their documents. I could see the separate room behind the counter where the dispensing room would be located.

It was perfect, and I had to have it.

Keeping my eye on my vision helped me enormously as I started looking for a space to launch my new business. But I also deployed another important strategy that's guided me to success: looking for and, more important, *trusting* the green lights encountered along the way. The first of my green lights came from Kristine, who saw the risk—the incredible leap of faith—that I was taking and decided to take one of her own.

My ideal building had a couple of very specific requirements. First and foremost, I wanted a freestanding building. The idea of sharing a common wall with another business just seemed like a recipe for conflict over three issues: odor, security, and parking.

Whether you find it heavenly or hellacious, there is no denying that cannabis has a strong aroma that itself is the subject of much controversy. The last thing I wanted was to wind up sharing a wall with a crotchety next-door neighbor who was on the opposing side of that debate.

Security is integral to any cannabis operation, and I needed the ability to make my business and its building's perimeter as secure as humanly possible without worrying what ears or conspiring minds might be lurking behind that fourth wall.

As any retailer will tell you, there is a direct correlation between abundant parking and a solid revenue stream. I wanted lots of my own parking, and I didn't want to have to fight that same crotchety neighbor for my future customers' share.

I was also looking for a building that was centrally located in a regular retail zone. I didn't want to be off in some obscure commercial zone that would make visiting the store difficult for customers. Additionally, I objected on principle to the idea that a cannabis store should be kept hidden away like a city's dirty little secret.

Kristine's building checked all of my boxes. Plus, it was pretty.

I knew the city planning department had tax records, and I asked the friendly lady at the counter who owned the Locust Avenue building. She gave me a name but didn't have a phone number. Fortunately, the internet supplied the number, and I was able to make contact with Kristine. When I told her about my proposed business and my vision during that first phone call, she agreed to a meeting at her building. While walking through the building, she explained that although her former tenant, LabCorp, had vacated the premises and moved their location, they were still under contract with her for another six months. She also informed me that they were even paying her above the current market rent. I was crushed.

With my heart in my throat, I listened to her ruminate about the advantages of releasing them early in order to secure a new, potentially long-term tenant, the whole time waiting for the "Thanks, but I'll pass." But it never came.

Not only did she agree to release LabCorp from their contract so that she could lease her building to me, but she agreed to a lower monthly rent that was more in line with the current market value. She also didn't require a deposit. I could not believe my good fortune. As my high school driver's ed teacher used to say, "If that light gets any greener, we can smoke it." If he only knew how apropos that comment would be to me in later years. Yep, that light was as green as they get.

The green lights are always there, and the Universe will always present them to you. Your job is to pay attention, watch for them, and, when you see them, step on the accelerator. Hard.

There will be times when you will need to step on the brake, of course. The red lights do come, but even they can be used productively. Use that red light as time to think, reevaluate, and fine-tune your dream. But don't let your foot get too comfortable there. Such paralysis—in the form of insecurity, worry, and fear—will mean the death of your vision. Trust that the green light will come again, and when that happens, you have to hit the gas.

Many years later, Kristine told me that I was not the first person to contact her about putting a cannabis store in her building.

"Then why me?" I asked her.

"You were so enthusiastic, confident, and well spoken, I decided to take a chance on you," she replied.

I remember that first day I met her in August 2009, standing in the unair-conditioned lobby of what would become 530 Collective. Sweltering in the Shasta County summer heat, she told me that owning your own business was always ten times harder than you expected, but that it was always better than working for someone else.

She was absolutely right.

To this day, I owe Kristine an enormous debt of gratitude. At a time when cannabis stores were all but unheard-of, she took a tremendous leap of faith in support of an unproven businessperson. She also told me that her attorney had tried to talk her off the cannabis ledge, advising her that renting to such a tenant could put her building at risk of federal seizure and forfeiture. She ignored him and went with me anyway.

The building was mine. She gave me the keys, and I was one step closer to making my dream a reality.

FINDING MY VOICE

Opening day, September 12, 2009, had arrived. The week prior had been a mad scramble that involved driving for two and a half hours to the nearest Ikea for lobby furniture and decor, cussing heatedly during the assembly of that furniture, hooking up the computer and printer for the reception area, meeting the security and internet companies on-site for installation of their respective equipment, creating patient intake forms, building the database for internal record retention and ID cards, and finally stocking the six-foot display case with the pitifully small amount of inventory the store could afford at the time: a few strains of cannabis flower, a jar of hand-rolled joints, and the brownies and Rice Krispies Treats I had made and wrapped myself. Most important, I had received 530 Collective's business license from the City of Shasta Lake and hung it proudly on the wall next to the California Board of Equalization seller's permit.

The finished space looked exactly the way I had envisioned it: the lobby was light and bright; the rooms were clean, contemporary, and inviting; the music quiet and soothing; the 530 Collective logo I had created was in as many places as I could put it, including on the black T-shirts that I'd had printed to create an employee uniform. Even the name "530 Collective" was intentionally nondescript, the numbers "530" being the area code for the greater part of Northern California and "collective" referring to a group of patients. The absence of the word "cannabis" or "marijuana" was also intentional; I wanted a clean and simple name. 530 Collective looked and felt like no other cannabis store of the day.

It was a Saturday, which meant John was off work and able to be there. There was no money to hire any staff, but one of his buddies, Preston Cross, was excited to be part of the process and had volunteered to help out. There also wasn't any money for advertising, but there had been some media coverage, and with cannabis having been a hot item on the city council agenda, there was fair community buzz about the opening.

We plugged in the neon "Open" sign and waited. And waited. For two full hours, the three of us sat around staring at each other, the new Ikea clock mounted on the wall ticking away the minutes. I wondered if I'd made a horrific mistake. Finally, that first car pulled into the parking lot. Elation! This was it. 530 Collective was off the ground.

Cannabis had given me back the joy of beautiful, uninterrupted sleep, and I had become a believer in its medicinal properties. However, I was still a newcomer to its regular use. With only fleeting nights of indulgence, I was still a stranger to cannabis. Ironically, it was this lack of familiarity that enabled me to envision a new type of store. It was also what led to a problem shortly after opening.

Because I did not come from cannabis heritage nor, unlike John, had I been a lifelong cannabis consumer, there were times at the beginning when I was uncomfortable—uncomfortable with how to talk about cannabis, how to fit it into the conversation. I knew the subject was highly controversial, and in 2009, I did not yet have the confidence that I have today.

I believed in the product medically without question. I had seen it work wonders in my own life. I also didn't feel that it was any worse than alcohol for those who want to use it recreationally. But I wasn't prepared for the awkward feeling I would get when, in the first weeks and months after opening the store, I found myself being asked a very simple question: "So, what do you do for a living?" I hedged. Or I gave a generic response like "I'm an entrepreneur." I was uncomfortable with the question and just as uncomfortable with the awareness of my discomfort.

But every day in those early weeks, I encountered more individuals for whom cannabis was a godsend.

"Mark" was one of 530 Collective's first regular customers, and I saw him about once a week when he would come in to buy joints. He did not like to shop when other people were in the store and would often wait to come inside until he saw that it was empty. He had a soft voice and a sweet nature. He was also very, very thin. I knew from his ID that he was in his forties, but he looked much older. As Mark became more comfortable with me, he started to open up. A doctor's medical cannabis recommendation never states the condition for which it is written, so I rarely knew what each customer was using cannabis for unless they told me. Mark eventually disclosed that he had AIDS.

He told me that unless he smoked a joint before a meal, the wasting syndrome that was literally consuming him would not let him eat. Sometimes, even with a joint, he could not always keep any food down. He shared his experience with Marinol, the synthetic THC prescription medication, and how, despite repeated assurances from doctors that it was the same as "pot," it did not work for him. The joints did, sometimes. It was heart wrenching to watch him grow impossibly thinner every week. Then, one day I realized it had been several weeks since Mark had been in. I never saw him again. It was easier to tell myself that he moved away.

"Doris" was a conservative-looking sixty-year-old. She had her own doctor's note, but she told me she was really shopping for her eighty-year-old mother, who was battling stage IV cancer. Her entire family had been opposed to cannabis for as long as she could remember, but they had decided to see if it would help their mom as a last resort. The chemotherapy had been unsuccessful, leaving her mom deteriorated and listless. Along with bringing back her mom's appetite, the cannabis also brought back her laughter. It was hard to say which was more valuable to the family waiting for the inevitable.

"Martin" walked into the lobby one day and wanted to know where he could find information on the negative side effects of cannabis use.

"The *negative* side effects?" I questioned.

"Yes," he replied, "I want to know exactly how bad it's going to be."

This was the first time I'd been asked this question.

I jotted down some websites that I thought he might find helpful, and he left. A few weeks later, he came back with some more questions, this time about privacy—specifically, what did we do with patient information. I explained the documents I was required to retain on any patient who wanted to shop in the store and that this data was not shared externally. When he came back the following week, he had a doctor's recommendation for medical cannabis. He told me that he had become addicted to OxyContin after undergoing back surgery two years prior. The addiction was tearing his family apart, and, despite being staunchly opposed to cannabis, he was willing to try anything to reclaim his life and keep his family together. His plan was to use the cannabis to get off the Oxy, then to discontinue cannabis as well. He wanted to get to a place where he didn't have to use any drugs, period.

I saw Martin for several months, when he came in to buy cannabis edibles. The last time I saw him, he told me that the cannabis had helped him get off the opiates; he had not taken any for weeks. Now it was time for him to drop the cannabis as well. He thanked me for being there, for my knowledge and support, and for helping him keep his family together, and then Martin made his exit through the 530 doors for the last time.

These types of stories never stopped in all of my eleven years as a cannabis operator.

I also came to understand the more varied ways people might use cannabis. We had many customers who were using it simply to unwind and de-stress at the end of the workday, to elevate their mood and feel better. I realized there was a therapeutic aspect to this type of use. It wasn't strictly medical or recreational, by definition, but by improving someone's quality of life, improving their well-being, cannabis played a therapeutic role.

Witnessing day in and day out the positive, life-changing impact cannabis was having on so many began to cast not only the product but, more significantly, what I was doing, in a new and different light. The concept of elevated customer service that I had envisioned before opening had evolved yet again into something even more significant: helping customers elevate their quality of life. It was because of those patients, my very first customers, that I started to become a genuine cannabis advocate.

And in becoming an advocate, I realized how important it was to not just champion cannabis; the conversation was bigger than that. More specifically, I began to see the importance of furthering the industry not for its own sake but to further its legitimization in our society; to both make it more accessible to those who needed it the most and to destigmatize the product and its industry.

More often than not, new customers who had never been in a cannabis store before came in fearful and nervous, like the cops were going to show up at any second and drag them away in handcuffs. Recognizing this fear in the customers was the first step, perhaps the most important step, in helping them. Once I recognized their fear, I would take as long as necessary to get them to a point where they noticeably relaxed. I did this by expressing gratitude for the City of Shasta Lake. This always caught them off guard. They weren't expecting me to speak highly of the city, and this surprise took their focus off their fear and also provided some reassurance. I talked about how welcoming the city had been to 530 Collective and how great they had been to work with through the opening process; I talked about how pragmatic the city council was with regard to the city's cannabis ordinance; I talked about some of the friendly visits we had had from local law enforcement officials; I started asking open-ended questions about their previous experience with cannabis. The longer we talked and the more I was able to draw out the customer, the more relaxed they became. Only at that point could we really start to talk about the store, the products themselves, and the reason for their visit that particular day.

Although I was able to assuage that fear rather quickly through conversation, I wished the anxiety didn't exist to begin with. I knew this apprehension could only be eliminated through legitimization. Once I saw their fear and knew the solution, my vision began to evolve and expand.

I started actively looking for local outreach opportunities in the form of community groups and organizations to join and support. I searched for local cannabis advocacy groups to get involved with but was disappointed due to the hostile and combative attitudes I encountered from other local advocates toward cities and law enforcement. I began to look for and join statewide advocacy organizations like California National

Organization to Reform Marijuana Laws (CANORML) and fledgling national organizations like the National Cannabis Industry Association (NCIA) and its later state affiliate, the California Cannabis Industry Association (CCIA). These organizations were doing solid work to change the conversation about cannabis, and they were my first entry point to being a part of that change.

However, I knew that if I was to try to further the industry's legitimization, I had to start with myself. Hanging on to any level of discomfort about what I did, and any behaviors resulting from that discomfiture, simply would not do.

I had discovered a new mission above and beyond just running a cannabis store: I wanted to be a part of the change that this industry so desperately needed. Knowing my customers and their fears and needs, I wanted to break down cannabis barriers and shatter the cannabis stereotypes.

The wrecking ball I would use would be my voice.

I stopped hedging my answer to that once-dreaded question; instead, I held my head up when asked what I did for a living, looked people directly in the eye, and said with complete confidence, "I am a cannabis operator."

LEGAL CANNABIS 101

There's no way to sugarcoat it: in the beginning, California's cannabis laws were a cluster_____(insert your choice of expletive here).

In 1996, California voters made history when they passed the nation's first medical cannabis law in the form of Proposition 215. While certainly groundbreaking in its passage, the ballot initiative was only three-quarters of a page long and woefully sparse on details. The lack of specifics ultimately ended up causing a hornets' nest of problems that no one anticipated. However, without its passage, the nation would likely not be teetering on the brink of federal legalization as it is today. Already the overwhelming majority of states now have some form of cannabis permissibility under their legal belts.

The intention of Proposition 215 was to provide safe and affordable access to those medical patients who opted for a more holistic way to manage their health. The bill alludes to a regulatory framework through its use of several key words like "safe" (which could be interpreted as both "safe from prosecution" and "consumer-safe products") and "distribution" (no interpretation needed). California had the opportunity in the years immediately following the passage of Prop 215 to continue to lead the nation's cannabis movement by answering the initiative's call and developing the country's first cannabis regulatory framework. While there may not have been a road map to follow from other states, California could have looked to the models used by the similar industries of alcohol and tobacco to figure it out. Unfortunately, the state did not.

Rather than do the necessary legwork toward regulation, Sacramento simply danced around the subject.

In the years that immediately followed the passage of Prop 215, there was absolutely no follow-up legislative work done on cannabis, and it would be seven years before the state saw its next cannabis bill. In 2003, the California legislature passed Senate Bill 420 (hats off to the Senate staffer who I'm sure jockeyed in line to get that number) in a pitifully weak effort to make good on the covenants of Proposition 215.

The bill created a flimsy and voluntary state medical cannabis ID card program that never really worked. In all my years interfacing directly with medical cannabis patients, I can count on one hand the number of state cannabis ID cards I saw, and with good reason: the card was voluntary; it added another layer of bureaucracy to the process, an additional expense; and it did not replace a doctor's medical cannabis recommendation, which was still perfectly valid as a stand-alone document to obtain use and grow medical cannabis. Most significantly, however, the vast majority of the patients I served simply didn't want to have their names in a government database for cannabis, especially in 2003.

A significant piece of cannabis policy arrived in 2008 when California attorney general Jerry Brown, the former and future California governor, issued his Guidelines for the Security and Non-Diversion of Marijuana Grown for Medical Use. Once you've choked down the incredibly cumbersome title to his document, it digests into a relatively easy eleven-page read that outlines a very loose regulatory framework for how medical cannabis operators could navigate within the confines of the law.

While more comprehensive than anything else produced by the state, these guidelines were still incredibly sparse. They created gaping holes in the supply chain in that many of the necessary commercial industry activities were not addressed—specifically: manufacturing, testing, and robust distribution. The document also didn't comprehensively address the authority of local government in relation to the state law. Finally, these were *guidelines*, not statutes; they were not law. However, they were better than what the state had up until that point.

Most significant to this story, the Attorney General's Guidelines provided enough structure for 530 Collective to secure a permit to operate from the City of Shasta Lake. It was under the cover of Attorney General Brown's Guidelines that California's legitimate commercial cannabis industry began to take root in the form of cannabis collectives and dispensaries (those words are used interchangeably with "cannabis retailer") that started to pop up throughout the state.

The cities that you would expect to embrace cannabis stores, did. San Francisco and Berkeley were amongst the first cities to draft and implement retail cannabis ordinances, with Oakland and Los Angeles climbing aboard the bandwagon as well.

Enforcement was a problem, however, particularly in the larger cities, with many seeing illicit and unpermitted retailers open up faster than they could close them. For example, for several years, Los Angeles had close to one thousand operating retailers despite having issued city permits for fewer than two hundred. It was a mess across the state, and nothing was uniform, all because Sacramento kept kicking the can down the road.

From a commercial perspective, the Brown Guidelines addressed only collectives and cooperatives, focusing on their retail aspects through the discussion of sales tax collection and permissibility of dispensaries. Consequently, retail was the only link in the supply chain that local governments were addressing as well. No one would touch cultivation or manufacturing, even though the local governments had to realize the products came from somewhere. Testing and distribution were not even on the table for discussion.

And for every jurisdiction that made the decision to allow cannabis retailers, it seemed like there were twenty that decided they did not want the burden of being the sole regulatory authority for the industry. Without formal state regulation and with only the flimsy Attorney General Guidelines, the end result was a mishmash of conflicting and contradictory cannabis policy throughout the state.

Hence, it was a cluster.

California would not see any significant legislative regulatory attempts again until 2014, when two bills would lay the foundation for the groundbreaking Medical Marijuana Regulation and Safety Act (MMRSA) the following year. The legislature's work in 2015 also became the cornerstone of California's recreational cannabis initiative, Proposition 64, which passed in 2016.

Although local bans and ordinances varied drastically from area to area, a trend that would continue even after the state passed Prop 64, a clear pattern emerged: the blue, progressive, urban areas were embracing cannabis while the red, conservative, rural areas saw almost unanimous bans. In this regard, the City of Shasta Lake was truly unique and a pioneer of the time.

Located in a staunchly red part of the state, Shasta Lake is a small city of only fifteen thousand people. A younger city, incorporated as recently as 1993, it has a fiercely independent streak with a strong desire to walk its own path, a path that did not always run parallel with its older, more sedate sister, the City of Redding. Shasta Lake wanted businesses, and they wanted jobs. To get them, they were willing to embrace out-of-the-box thinking with regard to revenue creation, which meant embracing cannabis.

In 2009, when Shasta County and its other cities were either banning cannabis retailers or else feigning apathy with regard to their operators—as was the case with the City of Redding at the time—the City of Shasta Lake took a leap of faith, opened its arms, and was one of the first conservative cities in the state to proactively draft a permissible ordinance for retail medical cannabis within its jurisdiction. The city was just as much a pioneer as the two retailers it welcomed. In 2017, the city revamped and expanded its retail ordinance to include every state-licensed activity within its limits. The city government held to this open-armed proactive mindset for as long as I had the honor and pleasure to be a part of the city's business community.

Perhaps most important, it was the City of Shasta Lake's pioneering outlook and its willingness to embrace cannabis early on that ultimately allowed me to be in a position to forge the advocacy work that had become so important to me and to engage in a meaningful way in support of the state regulations that were so desperately needed.

THE ACCIDENTAL EXPERT

The first months, and even the first year, of 530's operation were incredibly slow. While this downtime was not great for the revenue stream, it did have an upside: it afforded me the time to read and research the laws.

I spent countless hours on the internet. I read and analyzed the text of Proposition 215, Senate Bill 420, and the Brown Guidelines; I mentally devoured every applicable Health and Safety code that mentioned cannabis; I read anything I could get my hands on that explained cannabis law.

I scrutinized the 2010 *People v. Kelly* ruling that changed permissible cannabis cultivation limits; 2011 found me poring over the *Pack v. Long Beach* ruling that changed how cities could permit cannabis retailers.

If it affected the store or the patients, I read it.

Understanding the legal landscape around cannabis not only quenched my own thirst for knowledge but became instrumental in building and maintaining the customers' trust as well as establishing my credibility with local officials. I did not realize it at the time, but through my extensive absorption of California's cannabis law landscape, I was taking my first steps on the path toward becoming a resource to whom both groups would turn in the coming years as the industry and regulation continued to progress. Though the controversial nature of cannabis somewhat forced these understandings, thoroughly comprehending the legal landscape of one's industry is probably an all-around good business practice, regardless of your industry. As they say, knowledge is power, and I was absolutely able to leverage both in subsequent years.

Embracing the controversial nature of cannabis stores in the City of Shasta Lake meant that I had to be part of the conversation. I had to know what was being said by the powers that be, the local government. Attending both city council and planning commission meetings was requisite, as was speaking at them when appropriate. Prior to embarking on this cannabis journey, I had never gone to any government meetings. I didn't know what the hell was going on. Consequently, I needed to attend for two reasons: to learn the process and hear what was being said. I felt awkward and out of place but always stepped up to the microphone when there was an opportunity to speak. Despite having received an A in my college speech class, my voice cracked and wavered, and I said "um" way too many times, but I knew instinctively that I *needed* to speak. My store and my industry needed a voice, and the city needed to hear from both. Nervousness aside, I was always dressed professionally. I kept my tone respectful and my points succinct. In my conduct alone, I was setting myself apart from the vociferous cannabis "activists" who often barraged the dais with profanity and threats about their "rights."

At the early planning commission hearings and subsequent city council meetings for the City of Shasta Lake during which they discussed cannabis, a sticking point that came up in nearly every conversation was the incongruity between state and federal law. At the time, this was probably the greatest political and legal obstacle the industry had to overcome. I heard this incongruity again and again from the lips of community members who were against cannabis, city officials, and particularly the city attorney. Those on the opposing side of cannabis could not get their heads around how the hell it could be allowed at the state level while still federally illegal.

Even from my standpoint, I wondered how this could be and was intrigued by the conundrum. How was it that California voters could have passed an initiative that was in direct opposition to federal law? If conflict with federal law was such a big deal, then why was Prop 215 allowed to stand, legally?

In today's world, this argument against cannabis is hardly ever heard anymore, but in 2009, it was at the top of the opposition's list. I realized I had better understand it and, even more important, be able to articulate a sound counterargument.

The answer I found was so simple that I was shocked anyone was using the conflict between state and federal law as a legitimate anti-cannabis platform. As a nation, we have, right in front of us—both current and historical—numerous examples where states have enacted laws that are incongruous with federal law. In some cases, the federal law prevailed while in others, the states ultimately won; in still other cases, the country is still divided on the legal standing of social issues. For instance:

- LGBTQ+ rights
- marriage laws
- firearms and ammunition
- immigration
- reproductive rights
- voting rights
- environmental laws
- seat belts and motorcycle helmets
- alcohol and tobacco consumption

While it has its rightful place on the above list as it pertains to states' rights, cannabis is unique in that it is both a social issue and a commercial industry. Although alcohol, guns, and tobacco align somewhat with cannabis in their commercial aspects, the controversy is reserved for the end product only; no one has ever been up in arms (pun intended) about barley or grape cultivation or steel manufacturing, for example.

Cannabis alone is unique in that controversy abounds along every link of the commercial supply chain from cultivation to manufacturing, to retail sales, to consumption. Not only is there the controversy around its negative social justice impacts, particularly on people of color, but also the social controversy concerning a consenting adult's right to choose what they put in their body.

The Thirteenth Amendment to the United States Constitution grants states the right to pass and enforce their own laws that may, at times, be incongruent with their federal counterparts.

At the time, this seemed almost too simple.

Certainly, it could not be this simple when the opposing side was sounding such a strong hue and cry. Or was the passionate opposition to cannabis less about the legal standing of its laws and more about how it resonates with the individual?

Perhaps it is that cannabis strikes a deeper societal chord than seat belts. And in truth, isn't this the case for any set of activists, regardless of what side of the issue they're on? Each side always has opinions about which they are protective and passionate—even if those opinions are not always based on logic.

I certainly have my own opinions and beliefs. I don't like to have them ridiculed, dismissed, or changed. Be they right or wrong in the eyes of another, they are mine, and I hold them dear. For this reason, throughout my tenure as a cannabis advocate and operator, I very rarely spoke from the perspective of opinion. One of the only times I went public with an opinion was when I worked on the opposition campaign to Proposition 64 in 2016. While ultimately in favor of state legalization, I did not fall into the "at all costs" camp. There were enough flaws in Prop 64 (which to me was primarily written to favor big business over independent, grassroots operators), as well as it coming too soon on the heels of the legislature's MMRSA (California still hadn't regulated its Wild West medical cannabis industry, and adding the recreational-use dynamic was only going to complicate matters), that I threw my lot in with the opposition.

California voters felt differently, and in November 2016, California became the nation's fifth state to legalize cannabis for recreational use. Although I was on the losing side of that battle, I respect the electoral process and the will of the people. And that's that.

I always felt that given my position as a cannabis operator, my opinion was self-evident. No need to hammer home the obvious. Instead, anytime I spoke, I did so from a position of logic. I spoke about case law. I spoke about statutory law. I spoke about precedent.

I found very quickly that this gave people pause. They were expecting me to come out swinging by clamoring about my rights and trumpeting my opinion.

I never did.

I believe this is something that set me apart from other advocates and activists of the day. While this approach may or may not have given me any more credibility over others, what I noticed was the differing effect my approach had on the other party; it gave the person to whom I was speaking space to listen and contemplate without becoming defensive. The other advocates I had witnessed in action typically came at any cannabis dialogue with a combative tone and a chip on their shoulder, everything about them screaming an "us versus them" attitude. I saw no reason that a productive conversation couldn't replace that style of communication, and I adjusted my approach accordingly.

When someone comes at you with an opinion, it is very easy to go on the defensive and quickly present a counter-opinion. Certainly, this makes for engaging and oftentimes entertaining debate. In the cannabis arena of my early operator years, I found this approach counterproductive, and so I defaulted again and again to the position of sharing facts, sharing information, and offering safe cover for conversation under the umbrella of logic.

Opinions are wonderful, yet they are mostly unimportant except to their holder.

Keeping my public opinion out of the conversation served me well year after year with whomever I was engaging, be they other cannabis advocates, state and local lawmakers, or regulatory agencies.

This is a lesson I continue to apply to all areas of my life to this day.

THE WILD WEST

The hand offering the plate had dirty fingernails.

"Do you want to buy these for your store?" was the question that followed.

Glancing over the individual standing before me in the 530 Collective lobby, I couldn't help but notice that his overall personal hygiene was on par with those fingernails.

I politely declined his wholesale offer.

How could this be a viable distribution model?

Yet, this was exactly how California had decided it wanted its cannabis industry to function. While fundamentally flawed and full of inconsistencies, from 2009 through the middle of 2017, the supply chain and distribution worked like this: As a medical cannabis patient myself, I was lawfully permitted to form a medical cannabis collective (530 Collective). The collective was then in turn allowed to possess and reallocate to its members amounts of cannabis tied in aggregate to its member base. For example, if state law permitted each medical cannabis patient to possess eight ounces of cannabis and the collective had one hundred members, then the collective could keep a maximum of fifty pounds of cannabis on its premises to reallocate to its other members. This cannabis would come from patients who had cultivated their allowed number of plants at their home, harvested said plants, and then determined that they had a surplus of dried cannabis flower. This surplus could be made available to any cannabis collective (synonymous with "dispensary") of which the patient was a member for a monetary value or reimbursement.

While an absolute disaster of a system in almost every way, the system was fantastic in that it was incredibly easy for me to obtain product to stock the store's shelves. Nearly 100 percent of the products were grown and produced locally, and when supply ran low, it was a simple matter of calling "Joe," or whoever else was on the store's list of internally approved patient-cultivators, to see when he could bring more of that stellar Blue Dream that the patient-customers were so crazy about. He would usually have it on my doorstep within the hour. Yes, the holes in this system were chasmic, but replenishment was easy.

While California's vote to enact the nation's first medical cannabis law was to be applauded for its pioneering effort to change the cannabis stereotypes and allow patients alternative health-care choices, California was also the poster child for a failed commercial cannabis industry up until 2015.

The patient-to-patient model also had several less-than-charming quirks aside from wonky distribution. All operators were required to structure as a not-for-profit entity—not a tax-exempt entity, God forbid, but a fully taxed mutual-benefit corporation or similar.

Additionally, although the state law acknowledged that a loose framework for commerce was implied, operators could not call the exchange of money a sale or a transaction. Instead, it was a reimbursement: a patient shopping in the store was "reimbursing" the store its costs of acquiring the product, and the store was conversely "reimbursing" a grower for their time, effort, and expenses in producing a product.

The store was required to obtain a seller's permit from the California Board of Equalization and was also required to collect and remit sales tax to the state. But under California's oddly structured lawful medical cannabis framework, what I was doing could not be called a sale. That would've been illegal. This meant that all records had to reflect the proper terminology. Terms like "sales," "revenue," and "profits" were replaced with "receipts," and "accounts payable" was replaced with "reimbursements."

This was a silly game of semantics, but it mattered in the eyes of California's legal system, and I was vigilant with regard to any level of compliance, particularly because any sort of state guidance was so scarce.

California's patient-to-patient distribution model left the supply chain inherently limited, unstable, and weak. For the first seven years 530 Collective was open, third-party distributors didn't exist as they did not fit within the confines of California's medical law. The patient-to-patient model worked more like a farm-to-table model with the growers bringing their products directly to the retailers themselves. The traditional, third-party-distributor model didn't come into play until 2015 when it was first championed into legislation—to no one's surprise—by former alcohol industry executives.

Without mainstream distributors and without significant cultivation operations of its own, the store's shelves were completely at the mercy of whoever and whatever walked through. My then-husband John's two-light setup in his closet helped stock the store shelves every three months, but that was hardly a commercial facility, and even that was not consistent.

In Shasta County, there was no shortage of cannabis cultivation; in fact, there's no shortage of cannabis cultivation anywhere in California or any state. Quantity was rarely an issue.

Nearly every day, and depending on the time of year, some-times multiple times a day, patient-vendors would show up at the collective with their wholesale offerings: outdoor-grown flower, indoor-grown flower, concentrates (available as either hash or kief), and edibles, which at the time consisted primar-ily of baked goods.

The person to whom it fell to evaluate the quality of the cannabis flower samples was John. The man knew his canna-bis flower, and he was in charge of reviewing (read "smoking") the flower samples left by the patient-cultivators, a job that, he often joked, sounded much more fun than it actually was. Grain of salt taken, it was easy to see, even through the eyes of a nonsmoker like me, that the quality of the samples com-ing into the store varied dramatically. He kept track of what he sampled and made notes on which products passed muster and which didn't. That list allowed me to keep the store shelves stocked with what he had determined were quality flower and concentrate products. Without testing standards or recog-nizable brands, the quality the store offered was in the very subjective hands of the buyer, and John, being the cannabis connoisseur that he was, did an outstanding job.

The closed-loop, patient-to-patient requirement also affected whom the store could hire. In order to receive the state exemption from prosecution, any individual working in the establishment was required to be a medical canna-bis patient. In 2009, in a rural part of California with higher unemployment rates and lower-income demographics, finding good help was a challenge even for regular businesses, or so my local business colleagues had told me. I would struggle against the subsequent reduced labor pool for the next seven years.

Limited legally on one hand by California's closed-loop sys-tem and on the other by applicants who thought that working in a cannabis store meant that they would get paid to smoke weed all day, building a stellar team in those early years was rough, the revolving door of employees ever in motion. That you will find yourself drafting company policy prohibiting employees sleeping in the break room while not on break so that you can then enforce fair disciplinary action against said employees was one of the fine-print items I must have missed in my Cannabis Store 101 class. Oh, wait; I was living that class.

Quirks of California cannabis law aside, the operations of the cannabis store were relatively uncomplicated in those pre-regulation days and functioned with a deli-style sales model that is still used in some states.

The first version of the sales floor in the 530 Collective was frighteningly small, but other than that, it looked like any other retail space. The six-foot display case had a shelf for edibles and concentrates; the bottom of the case held several jars that could hold up to a couple of ounces of the flower. A digital scale set on top of the end of the case and the cash register completed the setup. It was small, simple, and decorated with contemporary furnishings from Ikea.

The jars could be pulled out of the case and opened for customer inspection, as the purchase was often based as much on the visual appearance and aroma of the product as on its effects. As the flower sold and the jars emptied, the "shake" (the outer leaves from the buds that had fallen off in the jar-handling process) would accumulate in the bottom. The shake would then be rolled into joints that the store sold individually. During the slow periods, the staff set up the joint-rolling station in the back office and made productive use of that time. I sat and rolled with them.

Now, I may not ever want to smoke one, but in all the years that we hand-rolled those joints, no one could keep up with me. Seriously. I was really fast. Using a little hand roller and papers purchased from the convenience store across the street, I busted out perfectly rolled joints faster than the seasoned smokers, much to their chagrin. I was constantly amazed with how popular those joints were. The customers loved them. We couldn't keep them in stock and eventually had to purchase bulk flower for the sole purpose of rolling them into "Js" since the jars weren't producing shake fast enough.

When the team came to me in 2015 and wanted me to buy them the $4,500 Tommy Chong–sponsored Knockbox, a clever little device that could produce one hundred perfect joint cones in about two minutes, I looked at them like they were crazy. Why couldn't they just roll faster? However, I rarely denied my staff anything they asked for, and I eventually bought it. The return on investment on that little machine was about three weeks.

In 2009 when I first opened, 530 Collective's jars could hold only a couple of ounces because that was all the store could afford to buy of any one flower strain in the first year. We were such a tiny operation in those days in comparison to others in the industry.

When the patient-cultivators came in to leave a sample or discuss business, they had their flower preweighed into one-pound units, usually packaged neatly in turkey oven bags. We had to explain that the store wasn't looking to buy a pound of anything; our budget simply didn't allow for it. Often the patient-cultivator seemed surprised, and some would pack up their bags and walk out. Sometimes, especially right after harvest, these guys came in with a giant duffel bag. They would toss it up on the counter, unzip it, and ask if I was buying "units." Gray-market cannabis at its finest! I knew those bags held up to ten one-pound bags of cannabis, and there I was, barely able to buy ten one-ounce bags.

I never even looked at what they were offering. I would just smile and tell them they were in the wrong store. They always left looking somewhat offended.

In those first months, the store might not even see ten customers over the course of a day. The four-figure capital investment involved in launching the operation had been divided pretty much equally between the attorney who set up the corporation, the first month's rent for the building, a few pieces of decor and equipment, and a smattering of product; there were no reserves. For a couple of months, the store couldn't pay rent until the fifteenth. Given how generous Kristine had been in letting me have her beautiful building, I felt terrible repaying that generosity with late payments. This guilt was completely self-inflicted since Kristine never complained, never made mention of it. She had been a lifelong entrepreneur herself, and I guess she knew that the road of any new business can be rocky, particularly at the beginning. Her relaxed attitude gave me confidence and strength. Sure, I was terrified and had many bouts with insomnia over those slow days, but I always found a way to pay the bills, and knowing that I wasn't going to be hounded for the rent helped me stay calm and just keep on.

In those first sixteen white-knuckle months, the gross receipts were under $100,000, well below expectations. The store was technically operating in the black, covering its own expenses, but every extra penny that came in was reinvested back into the operations, primarily into more products, both greater quantities and more diversity. None of the revenue went toward wages.

The bills at home were getting paid initially by John's income, then later by his state disability payments, and money was tight. So tight, in fact, that in 2010 when John faced unexpected legal challenges from his ex-wife, there was only enough money to pay his attorney or the mortgage, but not both. The attorney won, and the mortgage went into default; the house would ultimately be lost to foreclosure.

Opening the store in September was, in many ways, a poor strategic decision as it was right on the cusp of the cannabis

harvest season (meaning that anyone growing their own cannabis had all they needed), but the city had green-lighted the
business, and I'd found a willing landlord, so it was then or
never. In 2009, most of the cannabis patients in Shasta County
were growing their own supply as there had not previously been
stores available to provide them access to medical cannabis.
With the onset of harvest season in October, the demand for
cannabis flower from the collective dropped as patients simply
harvested what was growing in their backyards. However, having a store in town was a novelty, and we had one thing their
backyard couldn't supply: variety.

The retail consumer psychology that is deeply rooted
in all Americans, that expectation of vast variety no matter what we are shopping for, had begun to manifest in the
cannabis customer for the first time. A customer who had
grown their own OG Kush in their backyard would come
in for some bubble hash, something they couldn't make for
themselves. During their visit, they might mention how
great their harvest had come out and how happy they were
with it. But then they would notice on the store's menu board
that we had in stock Sweet Island Skunk that they remembered from "back in the day" as well as some indoor-grown
Blue Dream, the strain everyone was talking about. Feeling
nostalgic and adventurous, they would, of course, have to
purchase a gram or two of each in addition to the hash they
had originally come in for. Even though that customer had
plenty of their own product at home, they suddenly found
themselves spending seventy-five dollars at the collective
simply for the sake of variety. It was absolutely fascinating to
be on the ground floor watching this change, this psycholog-
ical shift, take place.

The shift happened rapidly to the store's tremendous
benefit. By 2011, the gross revenue skyrocketed to just under
$300,000. Employees were hired; the edibles line launched;

and the store was able to finally pay consistent wages to both John and me. While it was a relief to feel like the store was out of the woods, I wasted no time reveling in it. I was way too busy!

THE COPS

Shasta County Sheriff Captain Forrest Bartell was ice-cold. There aren't many people I've met who intimidate me, but Captain Bartell was one of them. An imposing hulk of a man, he took over the assignment of the Shasta Lake sheriff sub-station at the rank of captain approximately a year after 530 Collective opened. Word had quickly spread, as it does in small towns, that he was vehemently opposed to "dope."

I remember sitting across from him in his office the first time I met him face to face and wondering if he ever smiled; my next thought was that arresting me that day probably would have accomplished precisely that.

When I first spoke with Captain Bartell on the phone, I invited him to come to the collective for a site visit. He turned me down flat. He said unless it was a call for service, he was never going to set foot in my establishment. In an effort toward politeness, he told me that I was welcome to come meet with him at his office. I took him up on that offer, and I met with him in his office that same day.

It was a brief meeting, and I knew going in that I could not have high hopes of winning him over. My goal for the meeting was to simply make his acquaintance and demonstrate that I did not have horns, a rather humble bar.

The captain was professional yet frosty. He made it very clear that he was completely against my operation but also that he respected the will of the city officials who had granted me the permit. Being stuck between these two opposing realities, he crossed his arms over his chest, leaned back in his chair, and glared at me over the rim of his glasses.

I think even his mustache resented my presence.

I told him that I respected his position and could even empathize with the conflict the existence of my store created for the law-enforcement officials who had previously spent their entire careers chasing down cannabis and its operators. I asked him to extend my offer of a site visit to any of the officers within his ranks who might be interested.

He said he would convey the message, and I left his office with my tail between my legs.

I would learn in subsequent years that in many ways, Captain Bartell was a study in contradictions. The chilly cop exterior that made him so excellent at his job and intimidated the hell out of the fledgling cannabis operator sitting across from him well concealed one of the warmest hearts I have ever had the privilege to know; he would become the most unlikely of friends and, along with his family, a lifeline in one of my darkest hours.

But on that first day, he was anything but my friend. Daunted but not vanquished, I knew that somehow, I had to integrate law enforcement into my outreach plans.

In 2009 and 2010, I had no idea what other cannabis store owners were doing as far as direct law-enforcement outreach, but my instincts told me it was somewhere between not much and nothing. In some cities, the stores were not even permitted, so the last thing any operator wanted to do was draw the cops' attention. I decided to go in the exact opposite direction.

There was nothing Machiavellian about my outreach intention. I have never viewed the cops as my enemy. Additionally, it
was never my goal to change law enforcement's opinion about
cannabis as a whole; that seemed too daunting a task. Rather,
my intent was that the local force should see my operation as a
viable, permitted business like any other in town and that they
should see me as any other business owner. I had to personal-
ize both my store as a local business and myself as an individual. This meant outreach, engagement, and most important,
getting them inside the building.

Despite not viewing the cops as enemies and despite my
belief that my outreach was absolutely critical, I must admit
that it wasn't always comfortable. But the work needed doing,
and so I pushed my discomfort and nervousness aside and did
what needed to be done. I still wish cops smiled more.

Over the next couple of months, several deputies and ser-
geants came through 530 Collective's doors to see the facility for themselves and to hear my perspective on the industry.
They joked that their vehicles in my parking lot were probably terrible for business, and they were right. From where I
stood in the Collective lobby, I could see the customers' cars
slowing down to pull into the parking lot but then driving off
at the sight of the cop cars. The couple of hours immediately
after any law-enforcement visit were always slow as customers
were afraid to come in, thinking the store was getting raided.
Although the cop visits may have resulted in some missed
sales, the outreach was important to me, as I diplomatically
explained to customers when their curiosity got the better of
them and they came back.

The law-enforcement officials who made the effort to
visit the collective and see for themselves what the operation
was like were always appreciative of my candor. I explained
to the cops as part of their site visit that I felt transparency
was critical to both my operation and its ability to successfully

integrate into the community. I always made sure to thank them for their willingness to keep an open mind. They, in turn, were respectful and often offered suggestions to improve security. They also always made sure I knew that Captain Bartell sent them.

THE MOTHERLESS DAUGHTER

My mom took her own life when I was eight years old, the collateral damage of depression warring with an unhappy marriage, the complexities of which I cannot hope to understand. In that destructive wake, my younger brother, Rory, and I were left with a dad who, as a construction worker, was faced with the challenges of being our sole caregiver.

Within less than a year, my dad remarried, and my brother and I found ourselves with a stepmom, stepbrother, and stepsister. The reality of six people suddenly thrown together, most relative strangers with quite different personalities, and all spread across a wide age spectrum, was nothing like the TV shows.

The emotional turbulence and tension were rough on everyone. My new stepbrother, Rob, and stepsister, Amy, weren't thrilled about leaving their home and all they knew in the Bay Area to move sixty-five miles away into the country. My stepmom, Judy, wasn't exactly overjoyed at the challenge of raising two more children, young ones at that, and I'm sure my dad didn't enjoy his new role as mediator of family squabbles.

What I do know is that the tempest of the family merger perhaps most acutely affected a small boy and girl who had barely been given time to grieve, let alone understand or come to terms with, the loss of their precious mom.

I don't have many memories of her, and those that I do have are more like snapshots, quick glimpses of bright color and emotion focused on a special moment in time, that are quickly gone. Her name was Patricia (she was born on St. Patrick's Day), but everyone called her Teish.

I remember her as bright and silly; I remember her as warm and affectionate; I remember her as always having time for me.

I remember her as small and fragile, so easily broken.

My father could not have picked a more opposite person to marry when he chose my stepmom.

Maybe it was just the confusion of a blended family with kids aged seven to sixteen. Maybe it was confusion over what had happened with our mom. Maybe it was resentment over having to share our dad. Likely it was all of the above and then some. Abandoned first by our mom's final act of depression, Rory and I now felt abandoned by our sole remaining parent, left adrift in the chaos of the new family dynamic.

Straight out of working-class America, my family was not wealthy by any means, but we always had warm meals on the table, new clothes at the beginning of every school year, and there were always gifts from Santa under the tree at Christmas. Certainly, to some, having those things may seem like a luxury. Yet at the end of the day, it was not the gifts from Santa that mattered. It was the sting of my stepmom's disaffection, the chill of her indifference, that my brother and I felt in our bones. Looking back now from a forty-year viewpoint, I don't know that she knew how to be demonstrative. It is warmth, affection, and understanding that every child craves above all. And I felt their absence acutely.

My dad and stepmom were strict, and, to be fair, a lot of their stringency paid dividends later in life, for which I am grateful: the mandate that I get good grades meant that getting into college was easy; the requirement that I get outside and play after school rather than watch cartoons meant that I learned to embrace physical activity; completing the daily chores encouraged a work ethic; not being allowed to gorge on junk food meant that I formed solid habits around eating; holding me accountable for my actions led me to develop a strong moral compass. Those were all good, important lessons, some of which undoubtedly factored into my business success, which is why I give credit where credit is due.

And yet . . .

At their core, my mom and stepmom were incredibly different people, and I could not reconcile those differences in my mind or heart. I always felt torn between the two, like I had to make a choice. And I chose the ghost every time.

That my stepmom was living figuratively in my mom's shadow didn't help anyone. My dad never moved us from the house where my mom took her life, probably because he didn't want to create more turmoil in three lives that had already been turned upside down, and I can't imagine what it must have felt like for my stepmom to live in that house, to live with my mom's specter. I don't know if I could have done it.

Regardless of the reasons, our household was rife with conflict, resentment, and hostility. In the mid-1980s, my dad took up the monumental challenge of completing his college education. Working construction during the day, he enrolled in night classes at Sonoma State University. He graduated with his bachelor's degree in 1990, the same year I graduated high school. I know he made that decision to go back to school for the betterment of his family and suffered some grueling years grinding away at both the day job and night school, but it was the right thing to do, and I'm incredibly proud of him for achieving his goal. At the time, however, I was an immature, unappreciative creature and only saw that he was gone more than ever as a result. Consequently, the tensions between my stepmom and my brother and me worsened, invariably affecting our relationships well into adulthood.

I couldn't wait to escape to college in 1990. My stepmom wasn't there the day I finished packing my things and left. There was no goodbye, and I was glad. It would have only been awkward and insincere.

Through my college years and beyond, the relationship became even more stark and sterile, yet I kept hoping things would change, that things would get better. I kept hoping for the kindness and affection I had experienced from my mom to resurface in the relationship with my dad and stepmom— the child inside never stops wanting that—but that never happened.

One day in my midtwenties, I was with a mentor who, after listening to me complain about my fractured relationship and latest grievance with my dad and stepmom, asked me quite bluntly, "Jamie, why do you keep going to the desert for a drink of water?"

Stunned, I let that sink in. This was a pivotal moment in my life, a paradigm shift.

It was at this point that I began to realize that we are each the creator of our own reality, and as such, we must take responsibility for both the good and the bad that manifest during that process. This is a concept that I have continued to nurture and study in the classroom of my own experience ever since that day—a concept that can be hard to accept, but once accepted is both exhilarating and liberating.

We create our reality through our perspective, and that reality is reflected back through our lens. Change your perspective—change your lens—and you change your reality.

It may seem like a quantum leap to accept that it's that easy to change one's reality, so I again come back to the example of how we innovate as a global community. The starting point for all innovation is a shift away from seeing what *is* toward seeing what is *possible*. If that were not the case, we would never see advancement of any kind; we would still be living in caves. But innovation is an accepted process, an accepted truth.

Suddenly it doesn't seem so great a leap to take what is already widely accepted in the world at large and apply it personally; to take the accepted process of innovation at large and use that same process as a guiding principle, as a creative force, in your own life.

This philosophy was still incubating in 2009 when I opened 530 Collective. I knew I wanted to build my store in a way that was different, and I definitely had a vision of what was possible. I chose that vision over what was and used it to push the endeavor forward. Visiting cannabis stores throughout the Northern California region in 2008 and 2009, I saw what *was*. In my mind I saw the type of store that I wanted to create; I saw what was *possible*. Fueled by creative force, I was able to innovate my vision into physical manifestation.

However, I had not yet realized that this was an approach that I could apply to every aspect of my life. This philosophy—this approach to viewing my world—would solidify over the years as the stores became more successful and I honed my craft as a businessperson. In doing so, I was also honing my skill as the innovator of my life.

I gradually noticed that as I focused on my store's success and the directions in which I wanted to grow the business, those things became my reality. I came to realize that this was no coincidence. I was *creating* my reality; I was *creating* my success.

By shifting my perspective and focusing more on what was possible than what simply *was*, I was able to overcome some of my biggest challenges, both personally and professionally.

While I would further develop the aforementioned ideas over the subsequent decades, the seeds of that development were planted that day in my midtwenties when I realized that my dad and stepmom were never going be what and who I wanted them to be. And that really wasn't their shortcoming; it was mine. In failing to recognize that, in continuing to expect them to be what they were not, I was always going to be trapped and defined by them, by their perceived shortcomings, and even trapped and defined by the tragedy of my mom.

And what I wanted was to define *myself*.

The gulf between theory and practice can be vast, however, and change does not happen overnight. The residue of past hurts doesn't wash away easily, and the strained relationship with my dad and stepmom continued over the years. Yet because of that simple, profound question posed by my mentor, I had begun that day to view the relationship in a different way. As a result, I could maintain a relationship with them without being defined or hurt by it going forward.

I had learned a powerful lesson about choice.

We each are responsible for creating our world in which we can choose to play the role of victim or survivor.

We are each responsible for choosing a life of success or one of failure.

We are responsible for and in control of how we choose to see our world, the external as well as the internal.

I have clung to the memory of my small and frail mom, all while trying to avoid developing those attributes; I am her antithesis in many ways, which I consider to be both my greatest strength and my greatest weakness.

Many years ago, a friend told me that I am half dude.

What the hell did that even mean?

Not the outside, he had explained—the outside is quite feminine—but in the other ways, in my other characteristics that are more commonly observed in the male of our species: enthusiasm for beer, sports, and performance cars; an aversion to drama, gossip, and romantic comedies; and an inclination toward emotional unavailability.

The last of which will wreak havoc on personal relationships.

Allowing myself to be vulnerable—to be emotionally available—is still not something that comes easily for me. After a lifetime of running away from those feminine traits, I am now trying to nurture them, to achieve balance, and to accept all sides of myself so that I can be a whole person, able to both give and receive in a loving relationship. I am not an easy person to be with, but I'm always striving to be better, in everything and in all ways.

At the end of 2019, when my dad's condition took a drastic turn for the worse, my relationship with him and my stepmom, Judy, took a drastic turn for the better. In death's shadow, old hurts and wrongs, both real and perceived, finally wash away, and new perspective is gained.

The perspective and realization are that our time here is indeed very short and that we can, even at the final hour, choose to see the love that was perhaps there all along.

We can choose whom we embrace as our family. My brother, Rory, is my blood, my heart, and my constant inspiration. My stepbrother, Rob, and my stepsister, Amy—although we don't share a single common gene—are two of the most incredible humans I've been lucky enough to know, their love and support a blessing. They are my brother and sister, as much as Rory. They are the family I have chosen.

I chose the same with Judy. I now see the strong, determined, loyal, and intelligent woman who took on the huge commitment of raising my brother and me alongside her own children. I can choose to see that some of her greatest strengths are also mine, and I do not believe that is coincidental.

After four decades, the pendulum has fallen silent. I have achieved balance.

I *can* choose both my mom, Teish, and Judy. And I do so choose.

THE HUSBAND

No one ever expects to find themselves trying to wrestle a shotgun from their husband's hands so that he won't put the barrel down his throat and pull the trigger. Yet that was exactly where I found myself in February 2010.

I met John in 2008 when I was working for Pacific Gas & Electric as a community relations representative based out of Redding. I found him sexy in a dark, brooding way. My yellow lab, Rawley, it seemed, had a very different opinion. The day I took Rawls to John's house for the first time, he shied away from John, growling, and then pooped in the corner of his living room. I shouldn't have needed any more warning than that.

But literally for better or worse, I disregarded Rawls's advice, and after only seven months of dating, I married John in February 2009. Four months after our wedding, he told me that he was having thoughts of suicide. Being Captain Obvious, I suggested a counselor. He found one and started regular sessions.

By September, I had left my job at PG&E, and on September 12, 2009, 530 Collective opened its doors.

In another five months, just a few days after our first wedding anniversary, I found myself kneeling on the hood of John's running white Subaru, my shins burning from the heat of the engine, the downpour making it difficult for me to stay on the hood, and he in the driver's seat with the shotgun.

John had stopped seeing his counselor by then and had started experiencing increasingly frequent and severe mood swings. I witnessed multiple episodes of rage followed by bouts of silence.

I was terrified he would try to hurt himself; I was confused as to where this behavior was coming from; I felt helpless beyond measure. As if all those emotions weren't enough, the demons of my own past—my mom's suicide, the feelings of abandonment—were resurfacing with a vengeance.

On this particular day in February 2010, I was working at 530 when John showed up after his shift at work. I could tell immediately he was in a bad place emotionally. He stayed in the back of the store until it was time to close. We left together but in separate vehicles with him ahead of me in his work truck.

Dread latched onto my solar plexus and began to thrash about, slowly gnawing a hole in my core.

We got home, and John immediately went upstairs. I had a premonition that he was headed for the shotgun, and I was right.

He grabbed the gun and a handful of shells, shoving the shells into his pants pocket. I immediately tried to take the gun away from him, pleading with him to stop and talk to me, heedless of my own safety. He was just as heedless of my pleas.

John headed for the stairs, and I did everything I could to block his path. I knew there was no way that I could overpower him, so my strategy was to stall him, to wear him down to the point where he reconsidered his intentions.

We continued to struggle down the stairwell. Despite his best efforts to pull my hands off, I never relinquished my grip on the shotgun. Locked in that murderous dance, we descended the stairs and moved through the kitchen.

As John reached the sliding door, I grabbed onto his belt. He released the buckle, stripped off his pants, stepped outside into the pouring rain in his underwear, and got into his Subaru.

As he started the engine, I climbed on the hood. As crazy as it may sound, I didn't think that he would hurt me. I thought if I stayed on the hood, he wouldn't drive away knowing that I could fall off. I was partially correct.

I don't know how long we were out there, John sitting in the car and slowly turning the steering wheel in an attempt to dislodge me, and me, perched on top of the hood, staring at him through the windshield, tears mixing with rain, still pleading with him to talk. Whatever the length of time, it was enough for me to have burns on my shins the following day.

Eventually I lost my balance, and I slid off the car. He drove off, the white form of the vehicle disappearing into the rain like an apparition.

I realized, heading back into the house, that he had left the shells with his pants, but I did not know if there was one still left in the gun.

I called 911, and then I waited.

Eventually, the Shasta County Sheriff deputy showed up, and shortly thereafter so did John. The gun had not been loaded. After we talked with the deputy at length, he agreed not to take John on a 5150—the code that allows a law-enforcement officer to take someone into custody if they present a danger to themselves or others—if we promised to go immediately to Mercy Medical Center.

They kept him at the hospital overnight, releasing him at 6:00 a.m. the following day; I stayed with him the entire time. Physically exhausted and emotionally drained, I called a friend to open and run 530 that day.

I had hoped, after that agonizing incident, that John might take the necessary steps to get better, either through medication or counseling or a combination of the two. Unfortunately, he flatly refused to do either. He told me that he would use cannabis, and cannabis only, to treat himself. While I would later see cannabis work what may be called medical miracles for some individuals, this would not be one of those cases.

John did, however, decide to take a leave from work, and with the recent records from the hospital, he was able to get on state disability.

The subsequent weeks and months were a never-ending soap opera; some were good, others not so much. I never knew when the dark days would strike or what would trigger them, but they always came. Most of the time John was able to hold it together at the store. The customers and staff seemed to keep him in check. Nonetheless, I was frequently apprehensive about his interactions with both. Would a staff member or a customer trigger him? If so, what would his response be? Compounded by and likely resulting from my apprehension, our interactions were often strained, and I'm sure anyone in the building could feel the tension. Some days, whatever demons he was battling seemed to overcome him, and he shut himself in the back office. I never knew what he would be like from one day to the next, and that strain took its toll.

His behavior at home was even more unpredictable and often volatile.

He smashed windows in our house, broke the sliding door, destroyed furniture, and burned our wedding photos. Maybe his violent outbursts saved him from ever laying a finger on me. Or maybe I just don't know how close he came. It was terrifying, yet I never considered leaving him. At least not then.

After the rage would come the remorse. He would say he was sorry, that it would never happen again. He even begged me to leave him to spare myself from the hell he knew he put me through.

But I couldn't leave. I loved him deeply. He was my friend, and it was devastating to watch him going through this. I wouldn't give up on him.

My own emotions flayed and raw, my heart breaking, I took solace in the dogs, in the routine of caring for them and their unconditional love. Their whimsical personalities were balm to my soul. There were three of them by this point: my faithful yellow lab friend, Rawls, and two puppy brothers, Diesel and Boogie. In January 2009, John had met a guy outside a local grow shop who was looking for homes for the pups. He brought Diesel home that day. A couple of weeks later, Boogie joined him. Had I known what was to come, I doubt I would have thought adding two puppies to the mix was a great idea. That being said, I don't know how well I would have survived without them. At twelve years old, Boogie is still with me today, now a sedate senior citizen and, as always, my rock-solid companion.

I also found refuge in the store, its demands and the cyclical daily operations offering a kind of stability and welcome distraction from the emotional turbulence I was experiencing personally.

Throughout all this, I still showed up at 530 Collective almost every day and managed this fledgling operation. It was open seven days a week, 363 days of the year, and although the store traffic was slow, someone had to be there to run it. Balancing the needs of the growing business and the moods of a volatile husband was all-consuming, yet I was determined that both would survive.

In November 2010, nine months after the incident with the shotgun, I placed a second 911 call.

John had locked me out of the house, and, looking through the windows, I could see an empty bottle of Jack Daniel's, a box of Tylenol PM, and the kitchen table scattered with shotgun shells. Our butcher knife was on the floor by the sliding door.

I couldn't see John, and I couldn't see the gun.

This time it was not a regular Shasta County Sheriff deputy who showed up but instead two SUVs from the Shasta Lake Sheriff substation; they were Captain Bartell's guys.

The officers forced entry in flak jackets, their guns drawn. This time there was no discussion of my transporting John to Mercy Medical Center. They took him in on a 5150.

As they walked John past me, handcuffed on the way to the car, he looked at me with dead eyes and told me I was the worst thing that ever happened to him.

I never stopped hoping that John might change, that he might realize how much I loved him, how much I was there to support him, how much I wanted that to be enough.

But I was to learn that it would never be enough.

John was a bottomless pit of need that I could never fill. You never can love someone enough to make them better, to make them love you back, or to make them healthy. Love doesn't work that way. In fact, that really isn't love.

But I am stubborn and tenacious, and I don't quit. I hung in there, determined to show him how much I cared. The ebb and flow of his unpredictable behavior became the vicious cycle around which our life revolved for the next year and a half.

I didn't have a pattern of codependency in my past relationships, and I've never been one to stomach any amount of bullshit. So, what gives? Why did I suffer his appalling and toxic behavior? Because of my mom, of course.

John was resurrecting all those dormant emotions from my past, and I think the deep-down part of me hoped that if I could save John—if I could be enough, if I loved him enough—that would somehow ease the old hurt of not having been enough to save my mom.

My simple, child's love had not been enough to make her stay, but maybe this time with John, my complex, adult love would be stronger. Maybe this time I *would* be enough; maybe saving him might somehow make up for losing her. I was caught in an emotional vise from which I could not escape.

I couldn't give up; I had to try to save him.

Throughout 2011 and into 2012, 530 Collective saw rapid growth, with every month busier than the previous. I hired more staff, including a full-time manager; the operations expanded; and I launched both 530 Edibles and my staffing company in that time span. It seemed that the more successful the business was, the more things were falling apart at home. We were forced to be together during most of the working day. At home, we were increasingly distant with each other. The more I tried to reach John, the more he retreated. Night after night, we found ourselves sitting in the living room, each of us completely isolated, focused diligently on laying the mortar in our walls of resentment and hostility. I resented that he wouldn't talk to me or to a therapist, that he wouldn't take medication; he resented that I wouldn't leave him alone, maybe even resented that I didn't leave him, period.

Marriage is tough enough to begin with, but add a dollop of emotional instability to the mix and the situation becomes downright unlivable.

Yet live I needed to do. For me. Not being convinced that John would ultimately come to that same conclusion, I also had to keep going for the business. My brave face went on the moment I walked through 530 Collective's doors every morning and stayed put until I got home at night. The business needed me; the staff needed me; the customers needed me. I could not count on John, but I knew I could count on myself. If I had ever needed affirmation of my own ability, of my own tenacity, this was it. The lessons learned through this tumultuous experience were many, but the one at the top was that I will do what needs to be done; I will see it through. Following that lesson closely was the one that I will never again go into business with someone with whom I am romantically involved. No way.

In the middle of 2012, after some shitty remark I cannot even remember, I had had enough, and I left John.

He responded by finding a psychologist—a good one this time—and he started to do the work.

He said all the right things: that he missed me; he was sorry; he was himself again.

So he said.

After six months apart, hoping against hope and against my better judgment, I went back.

This time things actually did improve on the surface. John kept his appointments with his psychologist, "Dr. Z.," who is brilliant at what she does. I started to see her as well in 2012.

Dr. Z. is a literal lifesaver in every sense of the word, and she has helped me with both my professional and personal journey perhaps more than any other individual. While I started seeing her to work through the emotional pain John had inflicted, the ground we covered in session stretched well beyond. The scars that man left on my soul were fresh and raw, and they needed immediate attention. But, like most of us, I had older, well-hidden scars that needed attention as well.

Therapy is a journey of revelation, and it is also a journey of change. Often, we seek therapy as a result of some current crisis, as I did, and it is easy to point to that crisis, or sometimes another individual, as the cause of our turmoil. While this may be partially true, there is always more to it; there are always monsters in the deep, monsters that turn out to be our own reflection, a reflection of our fears, our past hurts.

Facing that reflection and coming to understand that it is in fact not a monster but an important part of who we are is therapy's holy grail: becoming the best version of yourself. Dr. Z. and I are still in touch today; she is one of my heroes.

On the surface, John seemed to be himself again, much as he was when he and I met in 2008; not quite, but close enough that I started to remember what happiness felt like.

When I decided to open the store, I knew I was naive about business, but I wasn't naive about the challenges that the decision would bring. I didn't think it would be easy, and I knew that I'd have plenty of obstacles to overcome. However, I had not bargained for having to tackle all the challenges that go with business ownership in parallel with incredible personal upheaval.

Perhaps the biggest takeaway is precisely that: That *life* happens in the middle of trying to run a business. Nothing happens in a silo. A million little distractions will worm their way into your landscape and disrupt your plan. Your job is to roll with it, to find refuge and solace in things that you love, and to stay the course. The undertaking of managing and running your own business is about managing your life as a whole. Your business and your life are interconnected—intertwined in a way that a mere "job" never is—and that is the very essence of what it means to be an entrepreneur.

EDIBLES AND ALGEBRA

In the midst of John's drama, 530 Collective was becoming more successful, with increased customer traffic and subsequently increased revenue. To support its continued growth, the store needed quality products, and from an operational perspective, I needed sustainability and consistency in the supply chain. Checking those three boxes for every product was challenging on the best of days in the preregulated California market, which brings me back to those dirty fingernails.

The absurd closed-loop model of distribution applied to cannabis edible products as well. As someone who used edible products exclusively and being someone with a very low tolerance, finding suitable products for myself was difficult. In the first weeks and months, I was the store's chef. My culinary skills are not great, but I could make cannabis butter and infuse a batch of brownies or Rice Krispies Treats at home in the evenings and wrap them prettily for the store shelves before heading in the next morning.

I found a recipe for the cannabis butter online, and I always made sure to make it with the same proportions of butter to cannabis. Even so, the effects of the edibles varied drastically as a result of the different potencies in the base cannabis that I was using, compounded by the effect of activating cannabis through the heating process, a concept of which I was completely ignorant in the first several years.

In 2009, there were no labs in the area to provide potency analytics, and mailing them samples was risky due to federal postal regulations and restrictions. The labs operating in the early years were fraught with challenges of their own, the largest being the lack of established baseline thresholds for contaminants like pesticides, molds, fungus, and heavy metals. To complicate matters further, different labs used different processes for determining potency, often yielding slightly different numbers.

Furthermore, none of the producers felt they should be responsible for testing their own products, regardless of the lack of baseline thresholds. In the preregulation era, the general expectation was that testing should fall to *retailers*, a completely ass-backward approach. I tried to encourage cultivators to do their own testing in exchange for fast-tracking to the top of the store's vending list, but they weren't having it. I tried the logical approach, explaining how it's not the grocery store's responsibility to test the alcohol content of the beer it sells; that responsibility falls to the brewery, winery, or distillery. Regardless of the product, all alcoholic beverages are required to be tested *prior* to arriving at the retailer. (Few of the producers with whom I spoke in that preregulation market felt that the alcohol model should be used for cannabis. California, however, would eventually follow the precedent set by its other industries and make testing the responsibility of the distributor in cooperation with the producer.)

With edibles, cleanliness was also an issue. For the edibles that were produced in a patient's home kitchen, I had to ask myself a couple of questions: How clean was that kitchen, and did the person preparing them have a food handler certification? In most cases the answers that I was forced to come up with were "not very" and "no way." In 2009, the local health departments had taken the stance that once a food item was infused with cannabis it became medicine and was consequently out of the scope of their jurisdiction. As such, cannabis edibles were treated more like a cottage-food item in that they could be prepared in home kitchens; the discretion as to the cleanliness of a particular kitchen was therefore left to my opinion of the vendor's fingernails.

When a patient came in with an edible product they wanted me to carry, I would always ask them how strong it was. The answers I received were varied; some were disconcerting; and all were completely subjective. I would be told anything from "Oh man, one bite of that cookie knocked me out for ten hours" to something like "Well, we used an ounce of pot in a pound of butter," which was a bit more informative, but still not helpful. There was simply no thought being given to dosage or consistency from batch to batch.

Consistency, or lack thereof, also applied to product availability. Occasionally, I would take a chance on a product and it would be a huge hit with the patients, as was the case with the homemade caramels produced by two lovely ladies who passed my visual hygiene inspection. Their caramels were individually wrapped in old-fashioned wax papers and came in cute little packages of five. They were delicious.

I did business with those ladies for several months until the day came that they stopped answering their phone. Customers who had been buying their product had gotten used to having them available. They were disappointed I was no longer carrying them, even when I explained that I was trying. This wasn't the only time something like this had happened.

As I sat in the back office one day in 2012, after making yet another unsuccessful call to the caramel ladies, I looked across the room and saw the adjacent kitchenette with new eyes.

Problems are easy to see and easy to complain about, but achieving success sometimes requires more than just overcoming a problem; sometimes success requires creating a solution. A simple solution to my caramel shortage would have been to source another caramel vendor. But that wasn't good enough for me. I wanted a bigger, stronger solution, a solution that had not existed before. I wanted to look beyond the obvious and innovate a viable, long-term solution to the problem.

The kitchenette had a utility sink and a counter. It needed a new stove and a bigger refrigerator. 530 Edibles was born. It was time to find a real chef.

I tapped one of our customers, and we got to work.

First, I developed a clear vision for what I wanted, based on what was lacking in the existing marketplace. I knew I had to look beyond my simple cannabis butter creations, as cooking with cannabis butter was a complete pain in the ass. It was smelly, messy, and it tasted terrible. Furthermore, infusing cannabis into butter meant limiting the range of products to those recipes that called for butter. My vision for 530 Edibles was different, bigger. I wanted products that tasted great *and* featured a diverse range of flavors and forms. To accomplish both goals, I looked into using concentrates, something few edibles producers were doing at the time.

Of the types of concentrates available to me in 2012, I chose kief, the dry, powdery substance that is derived from the cannabis trichomes, or resin glands, separated from the plant matter through agitation. It was easy to work with, and it was affordable. Once we'd found a source, my next goal was to establish consistent potency levels for every package the kitchen produced. This meant assuming the risk of sending kief samples to a lab for potency analysis.

Once I established the specific cannabis potency level I wanted per package—100 mg, for example—and once I knew the degree of potency of the kief, it was easy to figure out the number of pieces the recipe would yield and apply some good ol' high school algebra to calculate how much kief to add to each recipe. This was the one and only time in my adult life that I have ever used that high school algebra.

The 530 Edibles line was a huge success. The customers loved that they could get a bag of hard candy one week and when they returned the following, it was still available and the potency was the same. Customers could, for possibly the first time, buy edibles with confidence.

The products we started with were simple and ones we knew were already popular with the customer: hard candies, peanut butter cups, snickerdoodles, and the quintessential pot brownies. Rather quickly, the chef started to expand his repertoire into things like infused marinara sauce, ice cream, taffy, and even take-'n'-bake pizzas. I purchased a commercial refrigerator with a glass door, just like those in convenience stores, so that we were able to showcase the products in a way that kept them fresh. We used clear deli-container packaging as much as possible so that customers could see the products they were buying. Every container had a printed label with the product name, the ingredients, and the potency of the contents.

As the chef came up with more ideas about new products to try, my message to him (or her eventually) was always the same: You can make whatever you want. Once. The customers will determine if you can make it a second time.

The customers were always the gauge as to what items stayed in production as well as the items' production levels. Even knowing it was the most popular flavor and even with the chef cranking out batches nearly every day, it was difficult to keep the watermelon hard candy in stock. That was the store's all-time bestseller.

The products were incredibly popular. I knew going into this project that consistent availability and consistent potency were going to be game changers in the edibles department, but

I had not expected the demand to double, jumping from 5 percent to 10 percent of revenue, and that the percentage would continue to climb over the subsequent years. As word of mouth about 530 Edibles spread, the store started to pull customers from the other cannabis store down the road.

One unexpected trend was the increased demand for edibles around various holidays. The hard candies in particular proved to be a popular and, most important, discreet, way to de-stress during the frenzy of family holiday gatherings. Interestingly and yet not surprisingly, this same trend played out in 2020 during the COVID pandemic. Sales on edibles skyrocketed, and on several Monday mornings, the shelves were stripped bare of products. For those suddenly trapped at home with spouses and kids, gummies provided a convenient way to take the edge off and survive an incredibly stressful time.

Even with paying for the ingredients, the cannabis, the chef, and the packaging, the profit margins made sense. So much sense that I decided to take them to the next level.

In 2014, with a new chef who was fresh out of a renowned French culinary institute, 530 Edibles made its wholesale debut at HempCon, a two-day industry event at the Cow Palace in San Francisco. The edibles were all artisanal, and I'd invested in professionally designed packaging and a gorgeous website. I was ready for prime time, and I was rewarded for my efforts. The attendees of HempCon went wild for the products. No one had yet put a gourmet spin on their edibles line the way we had, and the raspberry bonbons and s'mores bars with dark chocolate ganache were in their own class. In the wake of the event, I promoted an existing employee to the newly created position of wholesale rep and deployed him to leave product samples with prospective accounts in the field as well as hand-deliver orders, a tried-and-true sales approach that was all but unheard-of in the industry in 2014. We were off and running!

Two of 530 Edibles' most popular products came about through employee innovation, albeit one of them by accident. Throughout its operation, the hard candies were without question the bestsellers. Very early on, the chef made the standard hard-candy flavors like watermelon, apple, cinnamon, and root beer. One afternoon, however, the chef came to me distraught, telling me that he thought the watermelon batch was ruined. Frustrated that our most popular flavor wouldn't hit the shelves that day, I asked why.

He told me that, being in a hurry, he had whipped out a batch of cinnamon hard candy and then immediately reused that same mold for a batch of watermelon. When he started to package the watermelon candies, he realized he could still smell cinnamon. Fearing the worst, he sampled a piece. Sure enough, the strong cinnamon essence had infused the watermelon candies.

"How bad is it?" I asked.

"Well," he replied, "it tastes like both cinnamon and watermelon."

I made that face.

He said, "Yeah, I know it doesn't sound good, but it's actually not bad."

I popped a piece in my mouth (of course, spitting it out immediately, not because of the taste, however, but because of my professional featherweight status).

It was delicious! Knowing that it would ultimately be up to the customers to determine the success or failure of a product, I told the chef to package it up and we would see what they thought. It flew off the shelves, and the flavor CinnaMelon was born. It was so popular in-house that it was one of the four flavors that we selected to roll out as part of the wholesale lineup. And all because of a glorious mistake.

The other bestselling item was the result of an employee's stroke of genius. Making hard candy by hand generates scrap product; the edges of the mold overflow a bit, and when the pretty pieces are popped out, there are shards left over. The shards, or scrap, are still delicious, of course, and, in the case of cannabis hard candy, still of value. The scraps were always saved, and the employees were allowed to take them home.

One day, one of my veteran employees, Mariah Johnson (née Henderson), came to me and asked if I'd ever heard of Belly Flops, the flawed Jelly Bellies that you can buy at a discount from their factory store.

"Sure," I told her.

She suggested we do something similar with the hard-candy scrap. She even had a name picked out for them: 53-Uh-Ohs.

"Brilliant!" I said.

It was a simple matter to weigh out the shards and format a new label. For the kitchen's convenience, we mixed up the flavor shards and sold the packages at half price.

They were an overnight success, and they were consistently a bestseller every week. When an individual feels part of the company—not just someone who works for the company—and when a team is empowered to offer solutions, the results can be brilliant.

During its peak, 530 Edibles had an extensive in-house portfolio of products and as many as a dozen wholesale accounts throughout the region. Our production was streamlined, efficient, and impressive, especially considering the small workspace. However, operating out of a one-hundred-square-foot kitchenette was viable only because of the lack of state or local regulation. Prior to the passage of the state regulatory legislation in 2015, the health department, the agency that generally oversees commercial kitchens, was hands-off with regard to cannabis operations. They took the stance that because the food items containing cannabis were considered medicine, production facilities and the items they produced were therefore out of their scope of jurisdiction.

With our professionally trained chefs and internal policies requiring anyone working in the kitchen to have their food handler certificate, impeccable cleaning standards, and following first in, first out (FIFO) inventory management, I was confident that our kitchen was cleaner than some restaurants I'd worked in. But it wasn't the same as a real commercial kitchen. I knew that the convenient loophole that allowed us to operate would eventually be closed by the coming regulation.

To keep 530 Edibles alive, I would have had to find a proper commercial space and outfit it with proper commercial equipment. With the increased traffic in the store itself and with the regulatory retail impacts that I knew were coming, I simply didn't have the bandwidth or the capital to move the kitchen and take it to the next level. Unfortunately, the edibles line would not survive regulation.

When I finally shuttered the kitchen doors in 2016, the chef was the first person in seven years whom I had laid off.

SMALL-TOWN POLITICS

While my community outreach efforts were successful in many ways, I encountered the occasional thorn. One of my very early community involvement endeavors was to join the Shasta Lake Chamber of Commerce. My intention was twofold: first, I was genuinely interested in the City of Shasta Lake and being a positive force within its community; second, I wanted to pursue any angle I could to legitimize my business, and I saw this as one of them.

The chamber seemed happy to have 530 Collective as a member and grateful for another business owner who wanted to get involved. I eventually found myself on the board of directors.

Initially, I was excited to be involved and had high hopes of accomplishing some positive work within the organization and of bringing new, engaging events to the city. I had expected to find the other members—those of both the organization and the board—similarly energized and motivated. What I found instead was an organization that seemed to be struggling on several fronts. At first, I thought these challenges and the subsequent discussions around them would be motivators for change. Yet the challenges seemed to dull the organization's overall appetite for change, and meeting after meeting yielded more of the same stagnation.

After months of frustration with the apathy, and in a moment of unbecoming self-righteousness over a unilateral and what I felt to be an inappropriate decision made by one of the other board members, I resigned. The situation that led to this moment is insignificant, but what is not is how I handled my departure. My letter of resignation was very pointed with regard to my thoughts and feelings regarding this one member and the situation.

What I would learn in the coming years, in the face of subsequent slights and snubs from certain members of the chamber, was that being so direct and open with my opinions in such a small town—particularly when the individual on the receiving end of my pointed comments was a retiree and a well-liked, active member of the community—was very unwise.

I suddenly found 530 Collective passed over on the invite list for and communication around community events, even events to which we had always been invited and in which we had participated in the past. My loyal assistant, Stephanie Pierce, the record holder of Longest Tenured Employee, was fiercely protective of the company, ever vigilant, and ever sensitive to these slights. When she noticed we had been left off the email or guest list, she diligently inquired with the appropriate contact as to why. Stephanie was always given a predictable excuse: they had meant to include us, but they must have sent the information/invitation to the wrong email address, or something similar. Stephanie, bless her and her heart of gold, was always the picture of professionalism and grace, accepting the apology no matter how many times she heard it before, and successfully secured our invite to the event.

I was, and always have been, very fond of the City of Shasta Lake community and even quite fond of all the members of the Chamber of Commerce. The barbs of rejection stung, but I knew it was my own doing. Pointed comments may sometimes have their place, but more often than not, their barbs come back to bite you.

I had learned a very valuable lesson: there is much power in the words left unspoken.

I gained nothing by my negative comments in that resignation letter.

In the first couple of months of 530's existence, I had gotten off on the wrong foot with a local leader by the name of Gracious Palmer, who served as both a city council member and mayor for the City of Shasta Lake.

We were both at a Shasta County Board of Supervisors meeting where one of the agenda items was a dispensary ban in the unincorporated areas of the county. She and I had both queued up to speak in the public comment period. I knew who she was, but we had never officially met.

Gracious spoke before me and, while at the podium, made a comment that both cannabis dispensaries in her town were run by men. When it was my turn to speak, I introduced myself and responded that clearly, I was not a man. Despite her error, she, rightfully, did not like being called out so publicly for her mistake, and her attitude made that quite clear when I tried to approach her after the meeting.

Our conversation did not go well, and I thought I had made an enemy for life.

Gracious was very active in the community; she had lost her reelection campaign in 2009, but she still went to all of the city council meetings as well as all the planning commission meetings. Our paths crossed often at these meetings, but she completely ignored me, and I made no further attempts at conversation.

She also attended nearly every community event I went to. I began to notice how much of her time she gave to the city, its people, and its organizations; she genuinely cared about the community.

We were very different people. We came from different generations; we had very different backgrounds; and we had different goals. Yet for all those differences, we were both driven by our desire to be a positive force in the community. Over time, I came to view her with the utmost respect.

In 2013, one of the city's seven planning commissioners suddenly resigned her seat. I didn't give the vacancy much thought, beyond the fact that there would be a new face at future meetings.

Nothing, therefore, could have surprised me more than the day my phone rang and it was Gracious Palmer on the other end, calling to encourage me to throw my hat in the ring for the planning commissioner appointment.

I was stunned.

After recovering from the shock of Gracious's phone call and giving the idea much consideration, I decided to pursue the appointment. I prepared my résumé and my letter of interest for the city council. I presented both documents in person at a meeting, and Gracious even got up and spoke on my behalf. The city council voted unanimously to appoint me to fill the vacancy through the end of its term, which was about seven months away. When that term was up, I sought, and received, appointment for a four-year term on the Shasta Lake Planning Commission. Gracious and I never spoke about our past differences. It was unnecessary, our mutual respect being self-evident.

Serving on the planning commission was an unforgettable experience. I learned volumes not only about the city itself but also about the public process—knowledge and experience that would serve me well in later years during my advocacy work on state legislation as well as throughout the statewide regulatory processes.

There are many ways to serve within a community: volunteerism, financial contributions, and organization membership. Having engaged in all of them throughout my cannabis journey, I can say with authority that the most rewarding community service I've ever done was serving as a city planning commissioner for Shasta Lake.

It is very easy, especially with today's hypersensitive, hyperpartisan political climate, to point the finger at the government, touting all of its shortcomings from our soapbox. But government work is hard, often thankless, work at all levels, from those who choose to go into electoral politics, to law-enforcement officials like Captain Bartell, to the individuals who volunteer time to any number of boards or committees.

I would encourage anyone who has a genuine interest in bettering their city or county to find a way to get involved in civil service.

You won't regret it.

THE THREE LITTLE PIGGIES . . . AND THE BIG BAD WOLF

Watching the surveillance cameras from the back office, I saw a man walk into the building and approach the reception desk. Carrying a clipboard and a thick manila envelope, he was clearly not a customer. A few moments later, reception phoned back that the man needed to see me. I walked up the hallway to the front in what felt like slow motion, my stomach sinking farther with each step. I knew what this was all about.

I signed the paper on the clipboard and opened the envelope, my hands shaking. The top of the page read, "The Superior Court, Shasta County," and below that was 530 Collective's name in the defendant box. The company was being sued.

In the fall of 2013, as I was settling into my seat on the planning commission, there was a disturbance in the 530 force. Seemingly out of nowhere, a seasoned manager suddenly developed significant performance issues. This was someone who had been with the company for a long time, someone I trusted implicitly, and someone whom I almost considered a friend. I couldn't understand why her performance and attitude had changed so suddenly.

After close to a month of trying to rehabilitate these performance issues, I was left with no alternative but to release her.

A few months after her release, she filed a complaint with the labor board, alleging a number of falsehoods. That complaint was later abandoned when she, aided and abetted—or possibly the other way around—by two other former employees and an attorney willing to take their case on a contingency, filed a lawsuit in Shasta County Superior Court seeking $250,000 in damages for a refined list of fabricated claims.

Being sued was another new experience for me, including the emotions that came with it: outrage was in the lead with indignation and unease in hot pursuit.

I needed a labor attorney, and I needed a good one. Enter another one of my heroes: Benjamin Kennedy of Carr, Kennedy, Peterson, and Frost. First and foremost, Ben is a brilliant attorney, and he wins. However, it would not be his legal skills that I ultimately came to value most. Ben is extremely direct, and, as a client being billed by the minute, I appreciated that directness. Second, Ben has an incredible sense of humor. In retrospect, I believe it was his cutting wit and blazing sarcasm that kept me grounded through the upheaval of the lawsuit, which ended up shaking up both my personal and professional life.

One afternoon in 2014, John and I were engaged in a heated argument about the lawsuit. I wanted to file a police report over some missing money that I suspected had been taken by the former manager who was now the leader of the lawsuit trio. I felt this had bearing on the lawsuit and should be reported. My attorney agreed, but John didn't. I didn't understand why.

I would not give in, and, faced with my tenacity that he knew only too well, he caved and told me that he thought he knew why the money had allegedly been taken. He confessed that in the summer of 2013, he had been briefly—how shall we say—dipping his pen in the company ink, the ink being the former manager with whom there had been sudden performance issues.

I've heard that hell hath no fury as a woman scorned. Amen.

That day in 2014, staring across the room at him in utter disbelief, everything suddenly came into focus. In that split second I understood the primary motivation behind the lawsuit and simultaneously closed my heart to John, knowing with absolute certainty that I was done with him forever.

I filed for divorce within a matter of days. I also filed that police report.

Despite his repeated pleas to forgive him, I never again had anything to do with him, and he never again had anything to do with the running of 530 Collective.

Even with my new, sharper perspective and with John out of the picture, the lawsuit was becoming more involved. Ben had to depose the three plaintiffs in his conference room, which meant I had to sit across the table from each of them separately over the course of several weeks and listen in silence to their lies.

The charges were all labor law based, and while fabricated—which scandalized me—none of the claims themselves were what you would call scandalous.

The day finally came when I found myself sitting in the conference room of Carr, Kennedy, Peterson, and Frost for Ben's deposition of the ringleader, the scorned woman. The plaintiffs' attorney—a disagreeable creature with a sour expression and chip on her shoulder—was present as always, her head down, taking angry notes.

Ben was making his way methodically through his labor law questions when he, without any dramatic pause, without even looking up from his legal pad, asked, "At what point did you begin romantic relations with Jamie's husband?"

The plaintiffs' attorney's head whipped up, and she looked at her client, eyes round with surprise.

She hadn't known about the affair. The attorney immediately asked for a break so that she could confer with her client.

We had found a potential weak spot.

But the case was far from over, and the suit ground on for months.

I was juggling a lot of balls simultaneously: incessant text messages from John, who was not taking the divorce well, the divorce process itself, running an increasingly busy 530 Collective and managing its growing staff, and analyzing the first cannabis bills to hit the California legislature in twelve years. I had recently become involved with two trade associations, the California Cannabis Industry Association and the Emerald Growers Association (later rebranded to the California Growers Association). Cannabis was hot in the capitol, and I needed to be part of the conversation.

I was the busiest I had ever been.

Making it a priority to be part of the process in Sacramento, I started to put systems and processes in place in my store that would allow it to run semi-autonomously, like a well-oiled machine, regardless of whether I was across the street in my office or across the globe. These processes were integral to the future of the company and an important milestone for me in that I had to let the staff take the reins. I had to trust them more than ever before, all while being sued by three former employees whom I had also once trusted. While incredibly difficult for me personally, I knew I had to get the store to a point where it ran without my daily oversight. I swallowed my personal discomfort and did what I needed to do for the betterment of the company.

With everything that I had going on, I was stretched very thin, and the emotional drain was tremendous.

It was no wonder I was awake at 3:00 a.m.

But of all the above challenges, it was the lawsuit that was responsible for the lion's share of those sleepless nights.

The injustice of their accusations hurt, but their lies—their deliberate maliciousness—coming from ladies whom I had hired and had genuinely liked, rankled. Had there been some merit to their claims, the lawsuit would have been easier to stomach, but the flame of injustice burning in me gave me strength.

Ultimately, it was because of those lies, and the malicious intent behind them, that I was able to eventually find solace, to realize a paradigm shift that would forever change how I dealt with crises.

That was when it hit me, again in the wee small hours, that it all came down to a very simple choice, which was becoming a conscious theme in my life.

I locked on to what I could control, and I was in total control of how I chose to spend my energy.

Staring at the words on this page, this sounds so simple. Yet the quagmire of distracting daily minutiae can be strong, and only by pulling free and taking time to breathe can one again see the forest.

My time each day was finite. I could control the time I woke up in the morning and the time I went to bed, but the daylight between those two points was all that I would be given that day. I needed to spend my daylight wisely. More specifically, this meant choosing to spend my precious energy and my daylight only on efforts that were positive and productive to myself and my business: exercise, staff training, new product education, customer appreciation, refining operational excellence, playing with my dogs. That last one may seem silly, but it is one of the main ways I ground myself. Then and now.

It came down to the question of what I wanted to give my attention to more. I could choose to spend my precious time and energy focusing on their lies, or I could get back down to business and focus said time and energy on my own success, the success of my store, and all the other important things that I knew needed doing.

Seen through that lens, the choice was simple: I wanted success more.

I let go of the negative emotions around the lawsuit; managing that circus, after all, was what I was paying Ben gobs of money for. I stopped focusing on the suit. I refocused on my company's success and the positive things in my life.

It was shortly after this realization that the lawsuit wrapped up. The attorney who had taken the case on contingency had subsidized it through a larger firm in Southern California, and that firm agreed to settle for a pittance just to get it off their plate, taking two-thirds of that pittance for their trouble.

Throughout the process, I spent more money on Ben than I did on the settlement. Significantly more. But he was worth it. Ben kept me grounded through an incredibly stressful process. He provided valuable advice on ways I could tighten up my businesses to make them bulletproof in the future, and he helped me learn how to be a better employer from a labor law perspective.

I never saw any of those three women again. But Ben I have kept as a dear friend because he makes me laugh and because he is a very snappy dresser.

My experience with John was unlike any I had experienced before in a relationship. And whether or not his volatile emotional state was simply an excuse for bad behavior ultimately doesn't matter.

John left deep scars on my heart, but, despite the havoc that he wreaked in my life, I've never regretted knowing him, nor have I regretted the experience of our marriage; he taught me a lot. Some of the lessons are obvious, of course. But I think the most profound lesson he gave me was in forgiveness. Not forgiveness in the forgetting kind, or the apathetic kind, or even in the karma-will-come-back-and-bite-him-in-the-ass kind, but in the choosing kind.

About a year after the divorce, while reflecting on all that was happening in my life and my current state of happiness, I realized how good—no, great—my life was. Duh, right? Of course I was loads happier living a life without John, but that wasn't the point.

It struck me that I couldn't simultaneously revel in my happiness while still carrying any sort of animosity or grudge.

You can't have it both ways, or at least I couldn't.

It was through that freedom of choice, the freedom that comes from looking both options in the face and consciously choosing happiness, that I finally embraced the true meaning of forgiveness.

CHURCH, JAMESON, AND LAUGHTER

The silveriest of silver linings that came out of my slowly imploding marriage to John was the friendship that I developed with the Bartell family. I believe it was because of those Shasta Lake officers who responded to my second 911 call that Forrest Bartell began to thaw and look beyond the cannabis and see me simply as a human being going through an intense personal crisis.

Forrest had done a lot of mentoring through his church, and he was well versed in being a shoulder for someone. Whenever I saw him at city council meetings or other community events, he always checked in on me. His concern was genuine.

At the peak of my crisis, when I had discovered John's betrayal, kicked him to the curb, and was struggling to find my bearings again, Forrest invited me to attend church with him and his family. An incredibly devout man, Forrest knew that I am a confirmed and lifelong agnostic when he invited me. I don't know if he really thought I would accept the invitation to attend the service, but I did. Several of them, in fact.

Whether an individual is religious or not, a calm unlike any other permeates the soul while one is in church listening to the sermon. Call it faith; call it the presence of God; call it inner peace—but whatever you call it, it was healing.

The shared Jameson was also healing. Not at the same time as church, of course.

During the winter of the divorce, the Bartells invited me to their home for dinner. They also offered me the use of their guest room as they lived an hour away and the mountain roads could be treacherous. Nancy barbecued rib eyes, and what great steak dinner isn't capped off perfectly with Jameson neat? Or the entire bottle?

To tell it true, Forrest and I consumed most of the bottle, laughing like loons, while Nancy and their son, Nate, observed our idiocy in amused indulgence from their chairs across the room.

It turns out it wasn't really the Jameson that was healing but rather the power of laughter and friendship.

Forrest retired from the Shasta County Sheriff's Office in 2017 after twenty-seven years of service, and the barbecue party held for him took place on a gorgeous day in April with hundreds in attendance. I had picked up his retirement gift while on a tropical island over spring recess: a box of cigars and a bottle of rum. However, feeling like he might need to *really* relax after all those years of service, I took the liberty of replacing a couple of the cigars with a couple of joints. Upon receipt of my gift, he immediately opened the box, homed in on the intruders, and asked in his sternest cop voice, "What are those?"

I smiled and shrugged innocently.

When I later asked his son what he ultimately did with them, Nate said he threw them away.

But in my mind, I like to imagine a different ending for those joints. I like to imagine that Nate dragged his dad and a couple of the other cops back behind the garage and instructed them in the finer points of puff, puff, give.

I'm not sure I can imagine a more unlikely friendship than one between a cop, his family, and a pot shop owner, but friendship isn't always based on similarities, and healing doesn't always happen when and where you might expect it. Our hearts recognize kindness, and our souls embrace kindred spirits, regardless of how unlikely the surface appearances. The Bartell family has been a treasure along this journey, their friendship an absolute blessing.

THE CAPITOL

When I was in sixth grade, I missed the school field trip to Sacramento to visit the state capitol. I can't remember why. The point is, I had never been to California's capitol building in Sacramento until January 13, 2015.

By this time, my marriage was over, but my commitment to my business and my employees had evolved into advocating for statewide industry regulation through the California Cannabis Industry Association, the state's first such trade association.

As a CCIA board member, I was part of its delegation to the capitol that January day. The association and its lobbyist had identified several key legislative offices for us to visit. These were legislators whom we, as an industry, expected to take up the challenge of regulating California's nineteen-year-old, rather unruly cannabis industry in the upcoming legislative session or who had a key role in the process that would impact any cannabis bills.

The previous year had seen the state's first two solid legislative attempts at cannabis regulation in California's history actually make some progress (Senate Bill 1262 by Lou Correa and Assembly Bill 1892 by Tom Ammiano). Although those bills ultimately died, the fact that they made it as far as they did through the legislative process meant the issue, if perhaps not yet the industry as a whole, was being taken seriously.

The unregulated "gray" market was spinning out of control and in many cases blending all too well with the illicit market. A few states had already legalized cannabis for recreational use and were well underway with their regulatory processes. There were a couple of freshmen legislators whose districts were significantly tied to the cannabis industry and who were prepared to take cannabis legislation seriously. Regulation was imminent.

It was imperative that the industry as a whole be part of the conversion in a significant way. Up until 2015, this hadn't really been the case. The industry had not yet developed its own voice, and, consequently, in 2014 and the years prior, the driving force behind cannabis regulation attempts was law enforcement. The California Police Chiefs Association was the only voice in the room, pushing for regulation that was, no surprise, heavily slanted along their bias.

As the saying goes in Sacramento, if you're not at the table, you're on the menu. The cannabis industry in California had to raise its voice and join the conversation to ensure that any significant cannabis legislation was balanced and fair; it had to provide a counterweight to the cops.

That lobby day in Sacramento in January 2015 represented a shift toward exactly that.

CCIA's lobbyist had set up office visits with several members of the Assembly and one member of the Senate. At the time, I could not have explained the difference between the two houses. Probably because I missed that school field trip.

California's capitol building is grand and beautiful, and I was completely awestruck. Walking into the building that morning and passing through the security checkpoint, I was in my usual speaking "uniform": size two black sheath dress from Banana Republic, three-and-a-half-inch neutral pumps, leather portfolio. Stepping my already five-foot-eight-inch frame into those heels made me nearly six imposing feet tall. With minimal makeup and polished hair, I knew I looked every inch the way a capitol political operative was supposed to look. But that was on the outside. On the inside, I was a jittery mess. Fortunately, I had been confident walking in heels since forever, but this was no time to get cocky. I decided to try settling my nerves by focusing on my steps. It worked. A double win.

What I also knew—and had known and capitalized on for years—was that I did not look the way people expected a cannabis operative to look. I knew this because I had heard exactly that from the mouth of nearly every individual I had met along my cannabis journey. The manifestation of the six-foot polished individual wearing a black dress in front of them was at complete odds with the ridiculous, tie-dyed, dreadlocked stereotype that was still, unfortunately, etched in so many minds, and I gloried in the juxtaposition.

I had found that when you catch people off guard in this way, you gain yourself an advantage. That disruption to their thought process buys you time: time to make your point that much stronger; time to shift the conversation in a direction you want it to go; time to allow the other person to begin restructuring what they think they know about a cannabis operator. This disruption was my secret weapon, and I planned to use it to its full effect in the capitol along with the rest of the impressive and similarly dressed CCIA delegation.

The first legislative member we met with was Assembly-member Ken Cooley, who had been vocal about the importance of California regulating its medical cannabis industry and expressed intent to build on the prior year's failed regulatory cannabis bill, SB 1262 (Correa).

An important side note: while the industry had shifted to using the term "cannabis," nearly everyone else was still using the word "marijuana," a slang term for the plant and product that has its roots in the racist sociopolitical propaganda perpetuated by staunch prohibitionist and first Federal Bureau of Narcotics director Harry Anslinger. The propaganda portrayed deviant and ridiculous behavior of Black and brown people allegedly under the influence of the drug and was intended as a fearmongering tactic to turn society against marijuana.

California's industry objected to the term and changed its name accordingly.

Although the groundbreaking legislation that was to pass in 2015 initially bore the objectionable word "marijuana," that term was later stricken in clean-up legislation in 2016, replaced with "cannabis," and there it stands today.

No one, at least in California, uses the term "marijuana" anymore in legitimate policy or industry discussions, a significant win that illustrates the important sociopolitical shift that has taken place in the state.

Back to Sacramento: in prior years, cannabis bills had been referred to the Public Safety Committee, which was exactly where law enforcement wanted them. The law-enforcement trade associations had a lot of influence over this committee and would therefore be more successful in amending any cannabis bills heard there to suit their views.

The industry did not agree with cannabis regulatory bills going to the Public Safety Committee and wanted different committee assignments for the new legislation we knew was coming. Specifically, we wanted input from the committees on Business and Professions and Agriculture.

While there were undoubtedly public safety issues surrounding cannabis, we, as an industry, did not feel it was appropriate that they be the *primary* committees to review cannabis bills. Law enforcement had a place at the table, but it shouldn't be *their* table. The industry would make its case—successfully—that a product changing hands for money was commerce and any policy regulating that commercial transaction should be sent to the appropriate committee: Business and Professions. Similarly, a plant that produces a viable crop is agriculture, again, something for which the state has a committee.

As I remember, while I was sitting in Assemblymember Cooley's office that morning, he came out from behind his large mahogany desk and perched himself on its corner. He looked relaxed, like he'd done this a million times, because he had. Our lobbyist introduced the association and its interests. We then were expected to individually introduce ourselves. As a group of seven to eight individuals, lobbyist included, the introductions took a bit of time—more time for me to sit there and sweat.

By this point in my career, I was a seasoned public speaker with no fear of the microphone. But this was different. This wasn't the same as speaking to a local volunteer group in a circle of folding chairs or at a fairground industry event; this was prime time. I felt my throat constricting and didn't know how I would be able to speak when it was my turn, but all my previous practice paid off, and I did.

I was inspired by how open-minded Assemblymember Cooley was about the industry and how positive he was about the need for California to regulate it. As I glanced around the book-lined office, I was completely overwhelmed that I could be sitting there, having such a direct and open conversation with a state lawmaker. With the California State Assembly seal dominating the wall behind Mr. Cooley and the plate glass windows offering views to the capitol building, it was an experience unlike any other. As I studied the view, I had a flashback to that nerve-racking opening day at 530 Collective five and a half years earlier and marveled at how far both the industry and I had come.

The second office we went to was that of Assemblymember Jim Wood. He sat with us around a large burlwood table in his personal office; he was dressed in a well-tailored wool suit paired with a muted yet elegant tie. He had impeccable manners, and as we each went around the table and made our introductions, he listened studiously, appearing very focused on what we each had to say. He was intense yet relaxed, the very picture of confidence.

Assemblymember Wood had just been elected in November 2014 to represent Assembly District 2. Prior to that, he had served two terms on the Healdsburg City Council and had practiced family dentistry. He was on the industry's radar because his district, AD2, encompassed the counties of Humboldt, Mendocino, and Trinity, otherwise known as that globally renowned cannabis mecca, the Emerald Triangle.

Starting in the 1960s, the Emerald Triangle began drawing cannabis farmers because rugged, sparsely populated terrain was also sparse on law enforcement. With the passage of Prop 215 in 1996, cultivation in the region exploded. Today it arguably produces more cannabis than any other region in the United States, both licensed and unlicensed.

Assemblymember Wood had also spoken publicly during his campaign about introducing a bill to regulate cannabis cultivation. He knew that this issue was a big one for his district, and he was driven, specifically, by the environmental damage caused by so many of the cartel growers, the worst of the cannabis actors.

With tightening restrictions all along the US/Mexico border, many cartels had discovered that it was easier to simply set up their own grows in remote parts of the state, often on public land. They used heavy pesticides long outlawed in this country, which made their way into waterways, critically endangering wildlife. Water from streams and rivers was often diverted to the cultivation sites to the detriment of those water sources. The sites themselves were usually heavily armed as well as booby-trapped against unwanted visitors. In fairness, it wasn't just the cartels that were engaged in this activity, protected by and under the guise of Prop 215. Plenty of US citizens both from California and other states were just as careless with respect to the environment, their illicit cannabis cultivation just as damaging. Regardless of who was doing it, the environmental destruction was egregious and had to stop.

Assemblymember Wood knew he could not control the negative environmental impacts without regulating the activity that causes it—cultivation—so he set out to do just that.

The next three legislative offices we met with—the offices of Assemblymember Rob Bonta, Assemblymember Reggie Jones-Sawyer, and Senator Mike McGuire, I believe—were selected because those members had also mentioned their intent to take up cannabis regulation as part of the upcoming session.

The day was a blur, culminating in a reception hosted by the California Cannabis Industry Association at the swanky restaurant Chops, directly across from the capitol, during which we saw a parade of legislators and staffers, some from that day's meetings, including Jim Wood—whom I couldn't get off my mind. All of them were interested to learn more about the CCIA and the cannabis industry.

As the weeks progressed, several cannabis bills were introduced and started slogging their way through the committees and the legislative process.

During this time, I divested from CCIA and aligned with a newer, smaller trade association, the Emerald Growers Association (EGA). It was exactly what its name implied: an association comprising primarily growers in the Emerald Triangle. Because I was a retailer, my involvement with EGA initially raised some eyebrows amongst the growers. But, unlike many other retailers, I was not vertically integrated, meaning I did not grow my own product to stock my own shelves. I was 100 percent dependent on the growers, the cultivators. My success was tied to theirs, and we were in this together. As a small retailer, I related more with the small growers. We needed to come together collaboratively rather than competitively, and the organization made us stronger and enabled us to speak with one voice. This is the very reason trade associations exist in the first place, but up until this point, there had not been such an association exclusively for the smaller, independent cannabis cultivators and retailers. We were in uncharted territory.

Growing rapidly in both scope and membership diversity, EGA rebranded itself later in 2015 to become the California Growers Association, and I became CGA's policy director. To herald its entry into the state political arena, the association hired Jason Bryant of Bryant Governmental Affairs to lobby on its behalf. Jason had been the head lobbyist for the California Dental Association for several years; he had substantial legislative contacts and a stellar reputation. While initially somewhat hesitant about taking a cannabis industry association as a client, he did. Taking this leap of faith, Jason became the second of only two lobbyists to actively and significantly engage with the California legislature on cannabis policy throughout the 2015 legislative session. The following year, there would be two dozen following in his footsteps.

Throughout the spring and summer of 2015, I spent about a third of my time in Sacramento. The systems and processes I had put in place at 530 Collective that enabled it to run without my daily oversight were holding. I built those systems on two principles: clarity and trust. I developed clear guidelines and set clear expectations; then I let management take the reins. I had implemented clear operational policies and procedures along with processes for disciplinary action if those policies were not adhered to. Management was empowered to handle any disciplinary situations that arose. The daily financial processes were set up with double verification so that every penny could be tracked and all individuals handling cash were held accountable. The systems for inventory replenishment were also spelled out clearly so that management knew exactly to whom to go for new products. I had created detailed budget formulas that told them exactly how much money they could spend on any product category. Management was empowered to create the daily break schedules for their shifts so that everyone got their meal and rest periods in accordance with labor law.

The entire team knew they could reach me on my cell phone at any time, but the managers also knew they were required to notify me only for something critical: a security incident of any kind, missing money over one hundred dollars, severe and unexpected inventory shortages, or any employee incident that may have violated labor law and/or resulted in termination. I was accessible, but I had also given them their independence. It was a tricky, delicate balance, but it worked.

I had an incredible team that I trusted, and they were well equipped to handle the increase in traffic that the store was experiencing. They knew what was going on in Sacramento and were excited that they, through my voice, were part of the conversation.

Progress was being made on the cannabis bills as they passed out of their respective committees. I sat through countless hours of hearings, pored over hundreds of pages of proposed legislation, and, each time a bill was amended, provided the CGA's executive director with ongoing analysis of the sections focused on retail.

Working through the legislative process, the industry as a whole, for the very first time, had a voice as to the edits and amendments we wanted made to the bills as they slogged their way through the process from committee to committee and from the Assembly to the Senate and vice versa. We were being heard, and we were being taken seriously. While we did not get our way on all aspects of the proposed regulations, neither did the other interest groups with whom we were often at odds. But, as any attorney will tell you, mutual dissatisfaction is the hallmark of a good negotiation. All the interest groups felt optimistic that we would emerge at the end of the session with the state's first regulatory framework for all aspects of the industry—cultivation, manufacturing, testing, distribution, and retail—and, most important, that such regulation would be balanced as a result of input from the various interest groups.

Indeed, that proved to be the case.

At the end of the 2015 legislative session, the several cannabis regulatory bills introduced had been boiled down to three: AB243, AB266, and SB643. All of them made it off their house floors with tremendous bipartisan support and onto Governor Jerry Brown's desk where, on October 9, 2015, that good man signed them all into law, thereby creating the nation's most robust, most comprehensive, most unique cannabis regulatory framework.

It had taken nineteen years from the passage of the country's first medical cannabis law in 1996 to the passage of the Medical Marijuana Regulation and Safety Act of 2015, but the industry was finally on its way to becoming a regulated powerhouse in California's economic future.

THE IRS

The mail had just been delivered to the reception desk, and I went up to the front to collect it. As I walked slowly back to the office, flipping through the envelopes, mentally noting the utility bill that would need paying and the junk catalog that would need pitching, I suddenly stopped in my tracks. There was something from the IRS, and it was suspiciously thin. This was nothing like their usual correspondence, which seems to have an entire ream of paper crammed into one envelope. I opened the letter and read it standing there in the hallway. The world closed in around me.

As the saying goes, nothing in life is certain except death and taxes. And possibly an IRS audit.

I may never know exactly how 530 Collective was picked for an audit, but it was. Receiving that letter in 2015 stating that the business had been selected and that I could expect contact from the local IRS office was heart-stopping.

In retrospect, I'm really not sure why I was alarmed. It was probably a knee-jerk reaction to societal preconditioning. I mean, I don't think there's a single person who gets all warm and fuzzy inside when they see or hear those three little letters strung together. A more common reaction might be slight involuntary regurgitation.

I had used the same CPA for all income tax filings, both corporate and personal, and she, of course, was the first person I called with the news. I may have been her first client to be audited. I know I was her first cannabis client to receive the honor.

She reassured me that she would be with me through the entire process, that it would be a process, and that we would just do our best. Easy to say when you're not the one in the hot seat.

As with any government bureaucracy, nothing happens terribly fast, and as much as I just wanted it to be over, I was in the unenviable position of hurrying up to wait.

The day finally came when I was to take the requested records to the local IRS office and meet with the auditor along with my CPA. She was a rock: smart, well-spoken, and most important, knowledgeable about the intricacies of cannabis tax law.

Never having been through an audit before, I wasn't sure what to expect, which was probably where some of the terror came from—that dreaded fear of the unknown.

I have been told I have a very expressive and transparent face, so I'm sure I looked as uncomfortable as I felt. Undoubtedly the auditor was used to this reaction from her victims. I honestly couldn't understand why anyone would want that job. Talk about a thankless governmental service.

The stereotypical auditor of my nightmares was a conservatively dressed, rigidly postured, prune-lipped individual with a perma-frown. But I learned firsthand how wrong stereotypes could be. As I sat there in the Redding IRS office looking at my auditor, I noticed the cute skirt she was wearing and her hip hairstyle. She completely contradicted my preconceived notion, and I was struck by a surprising realization: the auditor was a nice person. She was respectful and professional; she was thorough and direct. She made it all seem very black and white, which of course it was.

She told me I could expect the audit to last many months, maybe even up to a year (there's that slight involuntary regurgitation again). Not because she was spending all of that time entirely on my file, but because I was simply one of about thirty other victims—I mean, cases—that she was working on, and we each got about one day a month of her time.

One day a month for several months, maybe twelve of them. That seemed reasonable. I began to breathe again.

I have always been, in my adult life at least, an organized person, and my books for the store and all of its records reflected that trait. I had kept my records accurately, saved all my receipts, documented all transactions, both with the customers and with the vendors, and every penny going out or coming in had its paper trail. Everything was accounted for; it always had been.

As we got up to leave, I realized there was really nothing for me to worry about. The only real wild card was how this auditor would tackle the 280E issue.

IRS tax code 280E is the code by which any deductions for regular business expenses like rent, payroll, and utilities are disallowed if you are engaged in illegal drug trafficking. Since the inception of medical cannabis in the United States, the IRS has applied tax code 280E to all cannabis businesses, regardless of whether or not you're state licensed, because cannabis still remains illegal under federal law. Consequently, the fallout of 280E is that, without those substantial standard business deductions, the entity is taxed on artificial profits—profits that simply don't exist.

Unfair? Absolutely.

Unreasonable? Definitely.

Several battles over 280E had been waged in court, but the outcomes were not favorable to the cannabis industry. This is one of the industry's biggest challenges, even today, and relief will only come with full federal legalization.

The story of 280E's inception reads like an urban legend, or a really twisted fairy tale:

A long, long time ago (1981) and in a place far, far away (Minnesota), there was a drug dealer named Jeffrey Edmondson.

Jeffrey was a good, responsible drug dealer, and like all good, responsible drug dealers, he filed his tax returns with the IRS.

Because his little drug-trafficking enterprise was how he put food on his children's table (or jewelry around his escort's neck, perhaps), he claimed his go-fast boats, his mules, and his office on a Caribbean island as standard tax deductions (actually, I don't know what he claimed or if he used escorts; I just made those parts up) on his nice annual tax return and mailed it off to the big, grouchy IRS.

When the big, grouchy IRS saw this responsible drug dealer's tax return, it frowned and told him, "Oh no, Mr. Edmondson, you can't do that you silly, silly person. While you're required to file your returns and pay your taxes like all other happy Americans, you are naughty, and we can't allow you to claim deductions on expenses from your naughty, naughty drug business."

Well, our responsible drug dealer thought the big, grouchy IRS was mean and not playing fair, so he took it to court.

And, wouldn't you know it, the court was a kind court, and they agreed with our nice drug dealer man and said that he *was* allowed to claim all those standard business deductions (*Edmondson v. Commissioner*).

And Mr. Jeffrey Edmondson, the drug dealer, lived happily ever after.

The end.

Or at least it was the end until Congress got wind of this unacceptable ruling and created IRS tax code 280E in 1982 to prevent future drug dealers from following suit. Yes, that happened.

For the most part, this is where things still stand today. Thanks, President Reagan, for this legacy of your failed war on drugs.

There are now a few exceptions to 280E, and some deductions allowed as a result of hard-fought litigation, but by and large, 280E is one of the biggest financial challenges that any cannabis operator in the country faces.

In filing the returns, my CPA and I have always been mindful of 280E and have always played by the rules, knowing that those rules can change and that they are often subject to interpretation by the likes of auditors. That's what made it the wild card in the audit.

How would the auditor assigned to my case interpret 280E, and how would she apply it to the returns? Would she agree with our filings?

I will summarize succinctly by saying that in the end, after almost a year, and after the auditor looked at three separate years of tax returns, I got through the process. The company survived, and the auditor's adjustments were fair.

I'd say that's probably the best outcome one can hope for as the result of an IRS audit. The process was one that I can now

chalk up on my list of experiences, filing under the subcate-
gory of "Do Not Need to Repeat."

There was one more surprise for me at the end of the audit,
however. When the audit was wrapping up, she told my CPA
that my books and records were absolutely meticulous and that
had it been any other business besides a cannabis business, she
would've been done in a single day.

I have to admit that her unexpected compliment did give
me a warm, fuzzy feeling . . . kind of.

THAT ASSEMBLYMEMBER

Rewind to that day in January 2015 when I was sitting around the burlwood table in Assemblymember Wood's office in the California state capitol.

As I sat there, something happened to me personally that has never happened before or since (the "since" being much to Jim's gratification, I am sure).

I was captivated by him, and I couldn't pinpoint why.

I can't say that it was animal attraction, because although Jim is undeniably handsome, that was not what drew me to him.

It wasn't that he was well dressed, because damn near everybody in the capitol is.

It wasn't that he said anything terribly brilliant that day, although he is without question one of the most brilliant human beings I have ever had the pleasure to know.

It was simply that my energy responded to him in a way it has never responded to anyone else. It is not something that I can explain better even now, six years later.

At that time, neither of us was in a position to contemplate any relationship, and that was certainly not something on either of our minds that day; Jim was still married at the time, though I would find out later that he had been long contemplating ending his marriage, and I was coming off a recent and quite hellacious divorce of my own and still enjoying my independence.

So, despite my immediate visceral reaction to Jim's energy on that January day, it left as quickly as it came.

In fact, as the day progressed and my group carried on with the rest of the legislative office visits, Assemblymember Jim Wood was swept from my mind completely. Almost.

Yet he persisted. Not intentionally, of course, but over the next several months, my advocacy work in the capitol brought me into contact with him time and time again. I saw him in office meetings with CGA to discuss the bill he was working on, or in passing in one of the capitol hallways, or at an industry event at which he was speaking.

In June 2015, I was asked to be one of four panelists to speak on the status of cannabis regulation in Sacramento during a day-long cannabis event in Sebastopol, put on by the Sonoma County Growers Alliance. Jim had been a keynote speaker at several other such cannabis events earlier in the year, and I thought he might be on the slate for this one as well. To my disappointment, he was not.

But about halfway through the event, Jim showed up as an attendee. He wasn't there to speak but to learn. While not in his district, Sebastopol was not far from his home. I said hello to him, and we exchanged the usual courtesies. I was a familiar face, and we chatted for several minutes before he walked away to mingle with the other participants.

When it was time for my panel, the event organizers learned that the fourth panelist was a no-show. Word of Jim's attendance had spread, and the organizers quickly sought him out to ask him if he would fill in.

And just like that, I found myself seated next to him on the panel. Over the next couple of hours, I engaged in thoughtful cannabis-policy discussion, fielding questions from the audience, alongside one of California's premier cannabis legislators of the year.

During that panel, I also happened to notice that Jim was not wearing his wedding ring.

That event put me on Jim's radar. He was not quite as struck by my energy on our initial meeting as I was by his—it took him six months to catch up. But that's okay; my ego can take it.

Our relationship stayed strictly professional until the end of the 2015 legislative session and until after he was separated from his now ex-wife. Later, as our relationship evolved into something more than professional, we were free to move toward the future together that we both knew we wanted.

In 2016, I stepped away from my advocacy work at the state level to avoid any potential conflict of interest created by Jim's still being engaged in writing cannabis legislation. Although his bills only dealt with cultivation and never retail, we took no chances.

Every year, Jim has penned at least one bill on cannabis, tackling everything from regulatory cleanup language on cultivation to protecting the "cottage" growers to funding for environmental cleanup as related to unlawful cannabis activities, to the groundbreaking change in California's Controlled Substance Act that paved the way for Epidiolex, prescription medication from GW Pharmaceuticals that was the first cannabis-derived drug to be approved by the FDA.

To date, Jim has thirteen cannabis bills to his name, more than any other California legislator.

California had finally begun to legitimize the industry. The legalization campaign for Prop 64 was under full steam toward the ballot boxes, and agencies were gearing up to regulate this behemoth of an industry. However, after the 2015 legislative session, I never set foot in the capitol as a cannabis advocate again. I had found the statewide advocacy work absolutely thrilling; despite the work that remained to be done, I had to leave it to others.

In 2016, I refocused my efforts back on local governmental outreach, which had been somewhat neglected in the year prior. Cities and counties were now grappling with the state's sparkling new cannabis laws and needed help.

This work had always been what I considered one of the cornerstones of my success, and it was rewarding to reengage at the local level.

On a much more personal note, I found in Jim a partner of which dreams are made. For the past six years he has been my closest friend, my fiercest ally, my most trusted confidant, and my staunchest supporter, both personally and professionally. Without getting overly mushy, and keeping in line with this being a business book, I will simply state that it is my sincerest wish that those of you who decide to take an incredible leap of faith and follow your dream always have someone in your corner the way Jim has always been in mine (although this is also my wish for everyone).

CRAZY IS AS CRAZY DOES

In May 2017, Jim and I were attending a political fundraiser at Pebble Beach. I was just leaving the spa in a blissful dopamine haze when my phone rang. The screen displayed the caller's name, John Duckett, the city manager for the City of Shasta Lake. As he was not one to typically call me, I figured it must be important, so I answered. I could feel the euphoria evaporating as I snapped back to reality and went into work mode.

He asked me if I had heard about the letter.

"What letter?" I asked, the apprehension mounting.

And so began the chaos, starting with a letter to the City of Shasta Lake, in May 2017, in which a "Dr. Smith" expressed his concern over alleged tax evasion on the part of the city's three cannabis dispensaries: 530 Cannabis, Leave It to Nature, and Queen of Dragons.

Looking beyond the sensationalized content of the letter, the first and obvious question became, On what basis would a medical doctor, without any internal knowledge of or connections to these three organizations, be able to make such a strong allegation?

Precisely. Consequently, the letter had some credibility issues out of the gate—issues that one might think a highly educated individual such as a medical doctor might have foreseen.

Prior to the passage of Proposition 64, California law required that anyone wishing to use medical cannabis obtain an annual recommendation issued by a state-licensed medical doctor. The terms "prescription" or "script" were commonly used interchangeably with "recommendation," but technically, due to the federal status of cannabis, a doctor could not prescribe a Schedule I controlled substance, but they could "recommend" its use in the same way that they might recommend vitamins or an emotional-support animal.

Throughout the state, many medical doctors had chosen to make cannabis recommendations their specialty, serving the cannabis patients exclusively as opposed to engaging in general practice. There were upward of twenty such doctors in the Redding area, and for several consecutive years, I went to "Dr. Smith" for my annual recommendation.

I liked Dr. Smith. I felt he was more professional than many of the others I had encountered, which was why I kept going back to him. He was also, to this day, the only medical doctor who ever came through 530 Collective's doors for an educational tour. I held him in high regard. I saw him only once a year, and during those annual appointments, which typically lasted about twenty minutes, he was polite, respectful, and kind. There was never even a whiff of impropriety, malice, or instability in the air during the appointments.

However, since California had legalized cannabis in November 2016 and a medical recommendation was no longer needed, I didn't renew my recommendation in 2017.

Perhaps it was the ending of the medical-cannabis-dominant era as well as the financial profitability that went with it for the doctors who had chosen to make medical cannabis recommendations their sole source of income; perhaps it was witnessing my success surging on the tide of recreational cannabis—that of a lowly "pot shop" owner—into the mainstream while simultaneously causing his business model to drift into irrelevance, that triggered what appeared to be an unhinged downward spiral. The public documents on file with the California Medical Board tell some of the story; the rest played out as some rather disturbing conduct and Facebook posts for many months.

During that initial phone call with John Duckett, I assured him that the city was welcome to inspect my financial records anytime they wished. I also informed him that 530 Cannabis had rather recently undergone an IRS audit and that he was welcome to review those documents as well.

The city did its due diligence, and I believe the doctor's allegations were ultimately ignored.

He did not seem to take it well, as evidenced by his subsequent actions.

More letters followed, including letters to the Shasta County Board of Supervisors, the Shasta County Office of the District Attorney, and the Shasta County Sheriff's Office, all of which he started sharing on social media. I don't believe any of his letters received a response.

The doctor also began showing up at the Shasta Lake City Council meetings and pressing his concerns and implications during the public comment period. Despite being ignored, perhaps even because of it, Dr. Smith didn't stop.

He started posting videos, filmed in various locations, including inside his medical office, calling for boycotts of the three cannabis retailers, and attempted to organize picketing events at the stores. No one showed up to his events except him and his videographer. Shockingly, the doctor wasn't using his personal Facebook profile but was posting everything from his medical office's official Facebook page.

Over the next weeks and months, the doctor's videos and posts became increasingly more obsessive and nonsensical. At first, I didn't pay much attention to them. The man was flat-out wrong in his comments about me and my company, and I had better things to do. But my team was tracking him closely.

It appeared he was not getting the response he wanted, and his obsessive behavior seemed to be escalating. He started posting every day, sometimes more than once a day. My staff was becoming more concerned as the posts and videos became ever more bizarre. Then they told me I needed to see some of them.

The videos in particular were unsettling. They were of him, talking into his camera but rarely making eye contact with it. His face was shiny, as if from perspiration. His speech was fast, sometimes slurred and slightly incoherent. His location in the videos varied: some were clearly filmed at a house, some in an office, others in a vehicle, and others still in, oddly, what appeared to be a long hallway, like what you would find at a hotel. In many of the videos, he wasn't only taking aim at the three cannabis stores anymore; he was focusing on me personally.

He ranted about how I must have traded sexual favors for my appointment on the planning commission and that I must have bribed my way into a cannabis permit by paying off city officials. He ranted that I was poisoning—even implied that I was killing—patients by selling cannabis laced with pesticides. He sent Facebook messages to a couple of my managers, telling them that they were going to go to jail. (I suggested that my staff block him.) He went on and on about the three cannabis retail owners' missing money and hidden profits. In one video, he made reference to me allegedly hiding my millionaire status by living in a mediocre house in a middling neighborhood.

Yes, he knew where I lived. My address was part of my medical file, after all.

Had he just glanced at my address in the file and recognized the general area, or had he actually been to my house? That gave me pause. I couldn't stop his posts, and I had no way of knowing how often he had been to my house, but I could start documenting.

Facebook did not, at that time, let viewers save or share content outside of its own platform, so I reached out to our tech-support folks and had them set up a backdoor on my computer where I was able to download all of his videos directly from his page onto my laptop.

Having evidently been unable to gain traction with any of the local authorities, the doctor then started posting photos of letters he had written to Governor Jerry Brown, Lieutenant Governor Gavin Newsom, and Attorney General Kamala Harris. Sometimes he would re-create his letter into a post in proper letter format; other times he wrote in all capital letters. Although the subject of these letters was more of the same, his content was increasingly incoherent—like his post showing his diagram of where he thought all the missing tax money was going. It was difficult to read because many parts had been scribbled out or written over; other parts looked like they had been drawn using big colored markers.

After a few weeks, his posts started to veer away from me, focusing on other individuals and topics. He raved about his plan to start a new business, a strip club. He stated his intent to hold auditions in his medical clinic and set a date and a time for any prospective strippers to show up and try out. I had no idea if that was a joke, but it didn't feel like it. He was still posting all this on his medical office Facebook page; it was all public.

As if the audition call to strippers weren't enough, he posted a photo of what appeared to be his bare ass. The post caption read, "KISS MY TUSH . . ." and then listed city officials' names. Another post showed a package of Starburst positioned in place of an anatomical appendage between his bare thighs, his face smiling down into the camera, the photo captioned with "Want a STARBURST SHASTA LAKE CITY COUNCIL, RESDING [sic] CITY COUNCIL AND SHASTA BORAD [sic] OF SUPERVISORS."

Although I was grateful that his posts had pivoted away from me, I remained concerned about the continuing escalation and feared a worst-case scenario, particularly since there didn't seem to be any end in sight. People like this don't stop. They keep on, and they keep on until they get the attention they are seeking. That was what concerned me: Where was all of this going, and where would it end?

A few days later, when I logged on to Facebook and pulled up his business page, I saw a photo of him standing in front of the California capitol building. He was wearing a vibrantly colored tie-dyed T-shirt, and the hand that he was holding up to flip off the capitol sported chipped green nail polish. Also included in that post was a photo of the word "murder" and a photo of Adolf Hitler.

Later that afternoon, he posted a video of himself in what appeared to be the capitol cafeteria, calling on all escorts in the Sacramento area to show up to Jim's office and give him lap dances; the post also made several unoriginal and suggestive comments around Jim's last name.

The doctor even went into Jim's office as well as a couple of other members' offices. Jim's staff recalls that he sat in their lobby for about an hour even after being told the assembly-member was unable to see him. Jim recalls that his office notified security as to the doctor's presence in the building so that he could be on their radar. Ultimately the doctor departed the building without incident.

Then his obsession took a more menacing turn. He started posting pictures of bloody knives; he posted a text message meme about guns; the conversation seemed to imply both that he needed one and that he had one; he posted photos of the word "murder," written in what looked like blood. Even more threatening was the post that said verbatim (including capitalizations), "DEATH PENALTY FOR CANNABIS DISPENSARY OWNERS WHO did not test CANNABIS sold to CONSUMERS."

It seemed clear from many of his previous posts that the doctor saw himself as both judge and jury with regard to crimes he perceived were committed by me and the other two cannabis store owners. The terrifying question that arose from this new development was, Did he also see himself as executioner?

This was a whole new level, and it had to stop. Jim shared the threatening posts with the CHP, and I went to talk with Lieutenant Tom Campbell, who had taken over the Shasta Lake Sheriff substation upon Captain Bartell's retirement. Campbell was aware of the situation and had, in fact, been a target of a couple of Smith's posts himself. Campbell advised me to seek a restraining order, making him the second law-enforcement official to do so.

I filed for the restraining order—which doesn't prevent a dangerous person from doing something horrible, but it does give law enforcement more power if the order is violated. But I went a step further and compiled all of the videos and screenshots I had taken, and lodged a complaint with the California Medical Board. The complaint was an inch thick and included a USB drive full of all the photos and videos I had saved.

I had also been advised by several law-enforcement officials, including my dear friend Forrest Bartell, to get a firearm. Unfortunately, my being a cannabis operator made it a little tricky to exercise my Second Amendment right, so I opted for Tasers. I bought three.

In 2019, around two years after Dr. Smith began targeting me, I learned that the Medical Board of California had revoked his license. However, the board put a stay on the revocation, provided that he followed a laundry list of conditions showing rehabilitation progress as well as placing limits on his practice. All of these documents and findings are public record on the California Medical Board website.

Am I glad that the doctor was ultimately relegated to radio silence on Facebook and that I apparently ceased to be his target? Absolutely.

Do I take any comfort or find vindication in the disciplinary action taken against Dr. Smith by the California Medical Board? Absolutely not.

While I wish he had taken a different course of action to vent his understandable frustration, at the end of my experience with him, I am left only with empathy. The poor man clearly needed help. I hope he ultimately received it.

I tell the story of the doctor because it completely blindsided me. The other challenges I had faced, while daunting, were not terribly unique.

But the incident with Dr. Smith came out of nowhere. It was bizarre; it was unexpected; it was something that I never could have planned for. Even so, I had to keep going. Stopping was never an option. I had to continue to focus on the task at hand. Even in the face of the ludicrous, the unanticipated, the malicious, I focused on my vision.

SYNERGY

While impending regulation had closed 530 Edibles' kitchen doors, legalization opened the path toward new opportunities. As a result of the passage of California's adult-use initiative in 2016, more and more cities were considering cannabis operations, including Redding, the largest city in Shasta County, just a few exits down the freeway from 530 Cannabis, my newly renamed store. (I rebranded the store that same year since the word "collective" would become obsolete in the face of the new regulations, the company eventually being restructured from a mutual benefit to a stock corporation.)

Redding had a ban on retail cannabis in place for several years, but with the new law, a new city attorney, and new city leadership across the board, it was ready to look at incorporating commercial cannabis activities into its economy. Throughout 2017, 530 Cannabis hosted site visits to most of the City of Redding leadership. I was always transparent that should that city decide to allow cannabis retailers, I would be applying for a license.

I knew I wanted a store in Redding, and I thought it was highly likely that the city would allow stores in the near future.

However, I didn't know how I would come up with the capital necessary to open a store in the vastly evolved landscape of robust security and surveillance requirements, more expensive products, greater staffing expenses, more costly real estate, and last but definitely not least, the hefty state and local license fees. All I knew was that I couldn't do it on a wing and a prayer with a four-figure capital investment like John and I did in 2009. In 2017, 530 Cannabis was trending toward $3 million in gross revenue with fifteen full-time employees, and I projected that a Redding store would do, conservatively, at least that. I needed to consider outside investors for the first time.

As 2017 progressed, Redding moved its cannabis conversation along through three separate workshops, each focusing on the different aspects of commercial cannabis. I was one of the panelists on the dais during their retail panel, and I spoke at the podium at the others. I had also started my own conversation regarding investors with a consultant I had hired.

In developing a growth strategy for the new store, I was looking not only at Redding but also at the cities of Corning, Orland, and Goleta. With statewide expansion plans, it was unrealistic to think that I would be able to bootstrap multiple stores at both ends of the state.

I also needed a new brand. 530 Cannabis was a regional name and consequently a regional brand. It was also a brand in which my ex-husband still had a minority interest. With the new store, I was going it completely solo, and I had ambitions of eventually building out stores up and down California. I needed a brand that could have statewide relevance. I chose the name Synergy. It is a word we hear often enough, yet I doubt many see or realize just how simply beautiful it is. The word derives from the Greek *synergos*, which means "working together." Simple. Beautiful.

The word "synergy," as my shrink pointed out, also sounds a lot like "sin orgy." Leave it to the Freudian in the room to pull the sexual innuendo. However, the coincidence was innocent, and, in this case at least, a cigar was just a cigar.

I started working on the logo. I had my attorney set up another corporation, and I began to build out the business plan I would need for my investor pitch.

Redding's commercial cannabis diligence process was extensive. The months of informational hearings ultimately yielded a seventy-page draft ordinance that, after going through the additional public hearings and local approval process, was passed by the city council in March 2018. Their selection and permitting process was laid out in the ordinance, and it was rigorous. The city anticipated accepting retail proposals by June.

To submit a proposal to the city, I needed a location. There were only two buildings in the permissible zones that I was interested in, and my number one choice was not available to rent but rather listed for sale for $675,000. Unfortunately, I didn't have any way to buy it. Through the sheer strength of my reputation and with the help of the listing agent, I was able to get the owner to take it off the market and agree to lease it to me, contingent of course on my ability to secure a Redding permit. With that enormous obstacle out of the way, I started working on my proposal for the City of Redding.

A viable location was only the tip of Redding's proposal iceberg. The proposal also had to include the complete store layout, the available customer parking, any anticipated impacts on traffic, and the surrounding environment; the city wanted to know what systems I would use to control odor; they wanted a copy of my full security plan; they wanted to know how I would handle receiving products and distributors; they wanted to see design elements of the store, my timeline for opening, the number of employees I anticipated needing; they required a full business plan with financial projections, how much capital I expected needing to open; and finally, if investors were involved, they wanted their names and addresses.

When I finalized my proposal and submitted it to the City of Redding, it was 127 pages. I had not outsourced a single page. I had written it all myself rather than hire one of the numerous consultants who had suddenly cropped up in recent years, touting themselves as experts on California cannabis policy and selling themselves to operators unfamiliar with and daunted by regulatory language. Given that I'd been on the front lines of that conversation in 2015, I felt more than qualified to draft my own proposal.

The city set the proposal submission date for early June 2018. All applicants were to drop off their proposals (and the eight additional copies required) at the same time so that a city official could briefly explain the process that they would use to rank the proposals and how long they anticipated needing to decide. In its ordinance, the city had capped the number of permits allowed at ten, but officials had stated they anticipated that it would issue significantly fewer. There were eighteen applicants, several of whose proposals were thicker than mine. Competition was going to be fierce for the undetermined number of permits, and I could not assume I would be one of the lucky few. Longevity as an operator and my reputation were undoubtedly huge advantages in my favor. But I had a significant problem: I didn't have investors yet.

My proposal stated that I anticipated needing $300,000 in capital to get the store open the way I envisioned it and that I was looking to get a loan for that amount from investors. The proposal listed them as "pending." My venture capital consultant had made some introductions, and I had made my pitch months prior to submitting my proposal. A couple of them had even been to visit 530 Cannabis and had seen the proposed site for Synergy. I explained to my consultant that Redding was not going to award me a permit without knowing where my money was coming from and that listing the investors as "pending" on my proposal wasn't going to cut it. But still, they wouldn't commit. Time was running out.

When I was called in for my panel interview with the City of Redding officials, they kicked things off by asking what I felt to be the weak spot in my proposal.

Without hesitation, I replied, "My financing mechanism."

The heads around the table nodded in agreement.

I made an executive decision then and there.

I told them my financing plans had changed and that I would not have investors; I would be self-financing the entire project. They requested an addendum to my proposal outlining my new financing plan, which I emailed to them that same afternoon. I drastically stripped down the expenses and plans for the project to reduce my budget; then I itemized where I was getting the money. I used some of 530 Cannabis's cash reserves to fund a short-term, no-interest loan to Synergy; I did the same with some of my staffing company's cash reserves; and I used as much of my personal cash reserves as I could safely afford.

I showed the City of Redding how I was going to build out Synergy without taking a single investor dollar.

And so, on July 7, 2018, when Synergy was green-lighted as one of the six retailers to proceed on to the application process, I moved forward with the plan I had outlined in my proposal.

I terminated my engagement agreement with my consultant, pulled up my bootstraps, and marched forward under my own financial steam, one of the most empowering decisions I've ever made.

I had indicated in my proposal that my goal was to get Synergy open by September. That meant I had a lot of work to do in the next six weeks. I had to restructure the 530 Cannabis team to compensate for those who would be leaving to join Synergy. I had to interview, hire, and train new team members for the new store. All new Redding team members had to go through the background-check process with the Redding Police Department. The Synergy building itself needed a full remodel. I had to submit retail cannabis applications with both the Bureau of Cannabis Control and the City of Redding; their proposal process had merely cleared me to apply for a permit, but I still had to navigate their application process. I had to develop a budget for my buyer so that he could start setting up distributors to have on standby for delivery for opening day. I had to coordinate installation of security cameras, alarm system components, internet and phone, new door locks and keypads. I had to have the signage installed. And in the middle of all the nuts and bolts of getting Synergy off the ground, I had to make time for media and local politicians. It was a lot.

Below is the actual text reply I sent a good friend when he asked how the final forty-eight-hour lead-up to Synergy's grand opening was going:

> Getting there and it's going great!
> Today we had:
> Law enforcement's visit and training with our security team
> Councilmember visit
> Building inspection
> Water department inspection
> Planning department inspection
> Tech team connecting Wi-Fi access points and hardware
> Surveillance team installing phones and final security hardware
> Display cases stocked
> I had a snack, I think
> Unexpected trip to the City
> Reception area set up

Boogie got a drink from the fountain . . . again
Two customer groups showed up ready to shop
Mock transactions
Customer flow practice
Trip to Costco
Trip to Office Depot
Omg I'm exhausted
More meetings scheduled for tomorrow
Second building inspection for tomorrow
I think I sent a couple emails
I know I responded to some texts
Didn't sit down once
Got stockroom personnel organizing the Limited
    Access Area
Walkie-talkie protocol and lingo training
Cleaned up a homeless person's camp in the dump-
    ster enclosure and behind the building
Had an absolute effing blast!

I hit my target opening date of September 1, 2018, and Synergy was off the ground. In its first four months of operation, Synergy did $1.3 million in gross revenue. The following year, the store did just under $7 million and paid back all of its startup costs in the first six months of 2019. The significantly higher revenue was a result of the significantly larger population base in Redding, as well as Synergy's sales floor square footage, which was more than double 530's. It was a whirlwind from start to finish, and I loved every second of it.

Synergy had become Redding's first state-licensed cannabis retailer, and 530 Cannabis had received two of California's first ten licenses awarded by the Bureau of Cannabis Control. My stores and my team had successfully navigated the grueling transition from a Wild West, unregulated cluster to the most tightly regulated industry in California.

When Synergy opened its doors, we were, quite unexpectedly, the only game in town for the first seven months of our operation. I had figured that all but one of the other five stores that had been green-lighted at the same time as Synergy would be on a similar opening trajectory, but they weren't. Seven months provided a tremendous head start that definitely allowed us to build our brand and develop customer loyalty. But eventually the other stores began opening, and my staff members were nervous that the new competitors would take our shiny new customers. I wasn't.

I explained to the team *why* we didn't have anything to worry about. It wasn't because the competition wasn't real but simply that they were not our concern. We had our own job to do.

I coached them that rather than focus on the competition, it was our job to refocus on ourselves and to continue to do what we did best. I coached them to remember the reasons that we were there: to provide every customer a concierge cannabis experience, to be every customer's go-to for cannabis product knowledge, to simply be the best.

I never saw my pursuit of being "the best" as a competition, however. I didn't compare my efforts to someone else's as the standard; I simply set the bar based on my own expectations for and of myself and my businesses. Essentially, I was competing with myself, since being the best was and always has been about personal growth and challenge. I knew if I got up every day, kept my lens focused on doing the best I could in all ways with a constant eye on how I could improve, then success would inevitably follow. This was the culture I tried to promote and the attitude I hoped to instill in the team.

Since 530's inception, I never stopped looking for ways to improve the business and its operations. This was such a constant focus that I would tell prospective employees during interviews that if they were the type of individual to thrive in a dynamic work environment with lots of change, then they would probably love working for the companies. I always explained that some of the constant change was due to the flux in regulations, but mainly it was due to my figuring out new and better ways of doing things.

I was direct with the interviewees that how we did things today would not necessarily be how we did things tomorrow. I wanted them to know what they were getting into, but it was also important to me that they understood *why*. I wasn't trying to make people's lives difficult but instead to be staunchly committed to my never-ending pursuit to be the best.

Rather than worrying too much about what the other stores were doing, I encouraged our employees to focus on our own success, and our motives behind it; I coached them that our job was to, quite literally, mind our own business.

As a result, that was precisely what we saw manifest: our continued success even in the face of competition.

I never focused on my success at the expense of the competitors; it was never a choice between my success and theirs. I always believed that there were plenty of customers and business to go around.

I would acknowledge the competition's existence occasionally but only as an opportunity to evaluate my own operations: Were our processes as efficient as possible? Were our customers happy? Were we maximizing services to customers? Were we doing our best every single day?

Always keeping my lens focused on our own operations, on our success, as opposed to focusing on the competition is a nuanced, yet critical, distinction of perspective.

The universe is abundant, and I knew I could achieve all the success I wanted without it ever being at the expense of another.

That was my truth, which, of course, became my reality.

OUTREACH, SEXUAL REPRODUCTION, AND LUBE

I understood the controversial nature of operating my store in a very small town, so one of the things I did right from the beginning in 2009 along with law-enforcement outreach was community outreach. I operated under the presumption that while there might be folks in the community, particularly local government officials and law enforcement, who might be curious about my operation, none of them were going to come knocking on my door. (This was later confirmed when I was eventually able to secure site visits from them: several confessed to me that they were uncomfortable even parking their car in my lot during that educational visit because they were concerned people might think they were shopping.)

So, I went to them. I got out in the community and I went to meetings. I went to events. I joined the Chamber of Commerce. I participated. And while I was out in the community, I invited anyone and everyone to come see the operation for themselves. I invited members of the public, city council members, planning commissioners, and as was the case with Captain Forrest Bartell, the cops.

Without my really knowing it, something greater was taking place during these early outreach efforts: I was developing and fine-tuning the platform from which I would speak and the format I would use as an advocate throughout the rest of my tenure in the cannabis industry.

I always started with a brief summary of how I got involved with medical cannabis. I talked about my vision, and I invited the audience to ask questions—any question—particularly the hard ones.

I found that everyone had questions about cannabis, and those questions could run the gamut. My job was simply to share information. What I rarely did was share my opinion, that being self-evident and consequently not that interesting or productive. I was always much more interested in the questions and how those questions invariably evolved into an interesting and productive conversation.

In the earlier years, I saw these educational visits as opportunities for me to further the legitimacy of the industry. I never took my license to operate for granted. Consequently, in exchange for that privilege, I felt outreach was my responsibility and my obligation.

Undoubtedly, not all of my visitors agreed with what I was doing or, like Captain Bartell, were happy that I was on Main Street in their small town. But over the eleven years that I engaged in community outreach, every single visitor was respectful.

There's no way for me to know for sure how much my community outreach correlated with the level of success the stores achieved, but I believe it was significant. In today's cannabis industry, local government and community outreach is expected. But back in 2009, and even up until and through regulation in 2018, it set me and my establishment apart from the others, not only in my region but throughout the state.

In those early years, I was nervous, unpolished, and awkward—the result of taking myself way too seriously—and I don't know that those visits were incredibly fun for anyone involved. That really wasn't their purpose, of course, but over time, that changed. As various jurisdictions reached out requesting an educational tour, my naturally gregarious (and oftentimes cheeky) personality started to show itself more often. I began to relax, take myself (if not my operation) less seriously, and even find occasion for a bit of humor.

Many of the smaller jurisdictions that contacted me for educational visits had opened themselves up to the idea of cannabis in their community solely because of the tax-revenue potential. Shocking, I know. But money talks, and for small jurisdictions looking to fill their general-fund coffers, cannabis was enticing, and they had a Cinderella tax-revenue-generation story in the City of Shasta Lake, 530 Collective's hometown.

The city had placed a tax initiative on the ballot in 2014 to levy 6 percent of its dispensaries' gross revenue. The voters passed it by just over 60 percent (because the revenue was allocated to the general fund and not earmarked, only a 50 percent passage rate was required per California law). Several media outlets ran stories after the first year of collection. The $353,436 collected in the first twelve months was staggering for a small rural city of only fifteen thousand people, and the idea captured the full attention of other small cities in the region that were looking for alternate sources of revenue to replace lost redevelopment dollars. These other jurisdictions saw the City of Shasta Lake able to finally fill all its law-enforcement vacancies; they saw it able to support its business community in the form of grants and loans for business improvement; they saw the city able to tear down more of the blighted buildings within its jurisdiction as well as make additional infrastructure improvements.

Throughout the nation, with every election year, we see more states bringing commercial cannabis online, either in the form of medical permissibility or full legalization. While part of this trend is simply due to the significant sociopolitical shift around cannabis normalization, some of it is without question due to the economic drivers at play. Cannabis brings jobs; it fills vacant buildings; and it brings significant tax revenue. Even in California, some of the cities that had been initially reluctant to embrace the industry are now changing their tune because of the revenue potential. The City of Shasta Lake had seen the revenue potential and taken pioneering action in 2014, a full two years ahead of state legalization.

The subject of taxes is tricky, though. The industry doesn't want to be taxed at all, and the government wants to collect as much as possible. Somewhere in between is the sweet spot. Further complicating matters, as local jurisdictions seek to impose additional taxes on an already highly taxed industry, they run the risk of inadvertently promoting the illicit market, which is alive and kicking in every city throughout the nation, regardless of whether or not its state has legalized cannabis. Part of the proliferation of the illicit market is due to ongoing federal prohibition, but it is also due to states not building robust enforcement and eradication processes into their legislation or initiatives. States that legalize or decriminalize cannabis without such protocols make it very easy for illicit operators to grow and manufacture their products without fear of criminal ramifications. Those products can then be trafficked to states where cannabis remains illegal and therefore commands a higher price. Even illicit producers who keep their products within the state where it's grown can undercut the regulated market significantly and still reap a huge profit.

When states and cities impose excessive taxes on an industry in combination with exorbitant licensing fees that can skyrocket into the hundreds of thousands of dollars, while simultaneously failing to protect that industry against the illicit market by ignoring the illegal activity against which its regulated operators compete, you have a recipe for disaster.

California is a poster child for this exact scenario; in the five years since California's Prop 64 passed, we have seen our illicit market explode with the state taking little to no action against it. (This subject alone could fill an entire book.)

As long as the illicit market thrives—and make no mistake, it is thriving—there will remain cheaper retail options for customers. Consequently, states and cities must remain cognizant of this fact when setting their tax rates.

One such city was the City of Corning. Their city manager contacted me in 2017 after Prop 64 passed. Corning is a conservative city even smaller than Shasta Lake; yet the initiative had (surprisingly) passed within its precincts. In light of that apparent nod of approval from Corning's citizens, the city manager felt she needed to explore the possibility of a cannabis operation in the city.

By 2017, my media presence was prolific, so it was no surprise that she reached out to me. Over the course of several weeks, she and I coordinated no fewer than three separate site tours for their city officials and law enforcement. (Due to California's Brown Act, we could not have a majority of the city council present on any single visit. To avoid violating this act, we had to split up the council members into multiple tours.)

During one of these visits, the tour had moved to the back of the building, where we were looking over the clones, the baby cannabis plants that were available to the customers to purchase and grow in their own backyards.

I was explaining some of the properties of the cannabis plant, specifically ways in which the plant strains differ from each other. Not only are the plant strains unique amongst themselves but cannabis itself is unique in that it undergoes sexual reproduction, having both separate male and female plants.

One of the gentlemen on the tour then, of course, asked me the logical next question. "How do you tell the males from the females?"

My hand shot out from where it had been resting innocently at my side and made a very significant cupping gesture in the air while I said, "Well, sir, the males have pollen sacs."

I've always been one of those people who talks animatedly with their hands. (Thanks, Italian heritage.)

With my hand still kind of out there awkwardly floating in the air and my guests blinking at me like owls, I suddenly found it very hard to keep a straight face. I quickly turned away from the group and toward a more chaste area of the store, collecting myself so that I could continue the tour. Pollen sacs . . .

In December 2019, I found myself giving a similar outreach tour to officials from the City of Red Bluff. This time we were at my Synergy store, and along for the visit were the city manager, a consultant, and two law-enforcement officials—all men.

One of the law-enforcement officials, Police Chief Kyle Sanders, had been at 530 several years prior. The industry had evolved dramatically since then, particularly with regard to the development of the state's track and trace system, Marijuana Enforcement Tracking Reporting & Compliance (METRC), and significant changes to product packaging, as well as to the sophistication of the products on the market.

Prior to regulation, products had come into 530 in bulk. Cannabis flower, for instance, arrived packaged by the pound in Reynolds turkey oven bags. The flower would then be displayed in a jar for customer inspection, to be weighed out and packaged on the sales floor deli-style, based on how much each customer wanted to buy. Under new California regulations and the METRC tracking system, bulk product for retail sale was no longer permitted. Instead, it had to be delivered to the retailer preweighed and prepackaged in tamper-resistant, child-resistant, non-see-through containers with an associated blue METRC barcode that could trace that gram of flower or vape cartridge all the way back to the specific plant from which it originated. While there was nearly statewide mutiny by customers over this drastic change, I absolutely loved the bold move by the regulators. Cleaner and more organized, the new system made inventory management so much easier.

My tour group and I were on the sales floor, moving from department to department and discussing the types of products contained in each one. We eventually got around to the table that held many of the specialty products geared toward women, things like face primers, body lotion, and more.

I could have selected any product from the table that day, but the little devil on my shoulder chose the package of Quim. (Yes, there actually is a product called Quim, and it is exactly what you might expect with a name like that; it is lube.)

Holding it out for the group to inspect, I said, "I think it's just fantastic that today we have innovative cannabis products like this that can enhance sexual intimacy for everyone. And it's excellent for either solo or group play."

I stopped talking and paused for one heartbeat. Then another. And another.

Arms folded across bulletproof vests.

No one was making eye contact or taking the box.

Crickets.

There was an eclectic celebration of dance taking place inside me, but I kept it all inside. I simply put the box down and picked up an innocent CBD bath bomb, turning back to the group with a possibly not-so-subtle transitional comment.

"And this is another great example of a product that is *also* very popular with the ladies."

I bet that none of them forgot that tour. Outreach spiced with humor became my winning combo.

THE CASH

Heading into the fall of 2020, in the middle of a pandemic and toward the end of my tenure with the stores, the combined gross annual revenue of 530 Cannabis and Synergy was trending toward $12 million. All cash. Every penny, every dollar of that $12 million coming in was cold, hard currency. Think about that for a moment, and then consider that, even at their peak, my retail operations were on the smaller side for the industry. The cash burden within the industry is incredible. And it is scary.

Of all the concerns, responsibilities, and challenges that went into owning and operating a cannabis business, cash management and the subsequent security risks and safety challenges were always at the top of the list.

When 530 Collective opened in 2009, the industry was exclusively cash-only, and even in 2020, it was still predominantly so. In the eleven years that I owned the stores, neither had a bank account, but it wasn't for lack of trying.

In 2019, with 530 Collective in Shasta Lake still going strong and Synergy in Redding gaining revenue every month, I learned of two credit unions in Sonoma County that had begun opening business accounts for cannabis operators. Unfortunately, because these credit unions were local community-based organizations, they could not service my two stores two hundred miles to the north.

Over the years, I knew of some operators who had found banking work-arounds that ended up looking like a game of Whac-A-Mole. Operators would be granted an account, usually through lack of transparency, knowing from the get-go that its days were numbered and that eventually the bank would cop-to and close the account. But at least while it was open, the operator had banking access. I never opted to go this route with my stores. Constantly changing financial institutions was incredibly disruptive. With regard to my stores, I took the attitude of all or nothing; I wanted either full-access banking with full transparency or no account at all.

The cannabis industry's lack of banking access is a direct result of the federal law, specifically because all use, possession, or commerce with regard to cannabis is still a felony at the federal level. Accordingly, most financial institutions, being federally insured, do not want to be the middleman in a felony transaction. Even though federal financial regulators have loosened restrictions and begun to provide compliance guidelines, many banks and credit unions find the compliance requirements involved with taking a cannabis business client too overwhelming or cost prohibitive.

I have heard of countless banking "solutions" pitched to me by creative and ambitious individuals, and some states, California included, have set up working groups to try to find a solution to this problem. Upon in-depth study and scrutiny, however, all proposed solutions fail.

For example, in California, former Board of Equalization chair and current state treasurer Fiona Ma has been championing cannabis banking access since 2015, both throughout the state and before Congress. She and John Chiang, former

California state treasurer, have separately studied the issue extensively through public hearings, working groups, and outreach to boots-on-the-ground operators, including research around setting up a state bank or depository for cannabis operators. These are incredibly bright and accomplished individuals surrounded by the best of the best when it comes to data and analysis. Yet despite years of work, neither has been able to significantly open up banking for California's operators.

Colorado, the first state in the US to fully legalize cannabis for recreational use in 2012, has moved the banking needle the farthest by issuing a state charter to Fourth Corner Credit Union in 2014.

Individual states have the power to issue any financial institution a charter, which is its authorization to operate. However, to be fully functioning within the Federal Reserve system (i.e., to be a full-service bank), the institution must apply for and receive what's called a master account from one of the nation's nine Federal Reserve Banks as determined by their geographic region. When Fourth Corner Credit Union applied for its master account with the Federal Reserve Bank of Kansas City, they were denied, thereby hamstringing the bank's efforts.

The institution has since been in and out of court with the feds and is still not open for business. But Fourth Corner is not alone in the fight, and both Colorado and Washington now have a few financial institutions willing to bank cannabis money. However, even in those states, which legalized well ahead of California, most operators are still denied accounts.

Furthermore, the benefits of banking are not that helpful if you are the only operator with an account. For example, even if my stores did have checking accounts, the vendors to whom I need to write a $30,000 check for product can't accept it because they don't have an account in which to deposit the funds. The solution has to be broad spectrum, and it has to include all operators along all links in the supply chain. Shockingly, we are not even close to that solution.

Although on September 23, 2021, the US House of Representatives passed (for the fifth time) the Secure and Fair Enforcement (SAFE) Banking Act as part of a larger piece of legislation, the Defense Authorization Act. The package will still need to clear the Senate, something SAFE has been unable to do in the past as a stand-alone bill. Even if it were to pass out of the Senate and be signed into law by the president, SAFE would only protect banks from prosecution. Compliance requirements for banks and credit unions who choose to bank cannabis businesses would still be as stringent as they currently are given the fact that the bill does not legalize cannabis nor change cannabis's status within the Controlled Substances Act. The CSA keeps all cannabis use, possession, and commercial activities a felony. While it is an important federal step in the right direction, it remains to be seen if SAFE, assuming it eventually becomes law, will merely be symbolic or whether it will have positive and substantive impacts for industry operators.

The scope of this problem is tremendous. It touches every single cannabis operator in every single state in the country. This is a national problem, a problem that will truly be remedied only when the country sees full federal legalization of cannabis. Only through complete federal legalization will the industry have access to full-service banking, thereby removing the cash from the supply chain, which is really the ultimate goal.

In the meantime, it is up to every operator to come up with their own independent solution for how they deal with their lack of banking access and how they manage the cash.

An additional challenge is how a cannabis employer remits employee tax withholding and employer taxes. This is another of those fine-print items that nobody ever tells you about.

For example, when 530 Collective eventually began paying consistent wages in 2011, there were just a handful of us on the payroll. At that time, the company's employer payroll deposits to the IRS were below the $2,500 federal depository threshold that I did not even realize existed. When that deposit threshold was crossed, 530 received a congratulations letter from the IRS stating that because the payroll deposit and employer tax obligations were now over $2,500, the company was now mandated to pay electronically. There was no exception to this mandate.

Without a bank account, electronic payment of anything is impossible. I immediately called my CPA and asked her what I should do. Her solution sounded easy: "Hire a staffing company."

In contracting with a third-party staffing and payroll agency, that agency then becomes the actual employer of record, the obligation of employer tax remittance their responsibility and burden. A staffing company provides leased employees and support services, like payroll, for a fee, billing their clients for services rendered based on the terms of the service agreement. That sounded like a brilliant solution, and I immediately started calling staffing companies in the area.

But this was in 2011, and no one would take my business. Shasta County was, and still is, highly conservative at best and, in some cases, downright hostile to the industry. At this stage in the game, I was still an unproven operator with no connections, and the state was years away from legalizing. Looking outside the area to a more liberal, urban area for a staffing company wasn't feasible as that would have meant transporting the cash that I would be using to remit my payment for services. That didn't seem to make sense from both the efficiency and safety perspectives.

It was unthinkable that such a seemingly small technicality would be the end of the store, yet I had to find a solution. Taxes are no joke.

Since contracting with a staffing company was a viable solution and since no existing staffing company was willing to take my business, the obvious solution (in my unconventional mind, at least) was to start my own, and in early 2012, I did just that. Starting an entirely separate entity with all of the responsibilities therein, another company to manage and operate, all for the sake of being compliant with employer taxes, seemed asinine and unnecessarily complicated, which of course it was. Again, these are the things that nobody tells you about when you're at the grassroots level, building not only your business but also part of the greater process of building an industry from the ground up.

Complexity aside, it was a watertight solution with many additional side benefits that I would realize in the coming years. With a generic name, a non-cannabis entity, on their pay stubs, employees triggered no red flags when submitting proof of income for things like housing or car loans; the staffing company was able to secure lines of credit; it could handle multiple clients, multiple stores; and most significantly, it could get a bank account, thereby enabling it to comply with the IRS's electronic deposit requirement. However, the cash was a burden for the staffing company as well. It received payment for services rendered in cash, which was then deposited into the bank, which the bank didn't like. In a world of digital and electronic currency, cash is suspect, and eventually, whatever bank or credit union I was with would close the account.

In the eight years that I operated the staffing company, I went through eight financial institutions before finally, in my last year, finding a ninth that was comfortable taking the cash deposits, even knowing it came from cannabis clients: Community First Credit Union in Santa Rosa.

Establishing my own staffing company solved the problem of employer-tax obligations, but there was still all that cash to deal with, and its management alone was overwhelming. Many have told me it's a great problem to have, and while I can't disagree, it was still a problem, and I took the solutions very seriously.

For the first years, I was the one primarily in charge of cash handling and cash-management systems. But as the business grew and as I stopped spending seven days a week, opening to closing, at the store, I had to trust others. I couldn't physically touch every dollar, but I'd have to track each one.

The tracking systems I put in place initially were rudimentary, but they served, and, as more money came in and more fingers started touching it, I revised and sharpened those systems. The years 2014 and 2015 were pivotal with regard to refining the overall policies and procedures, since I was spending so much time engaged in the legislative process in Sacramento. In order for the stores to run successfully without my daily oversight, I had to develop systems to not only double- and triple-verify every dollar coming in and going out but also systems to double- and triple-verify the *verifiers*.

It was a constant work in progress that involved a lot of trial and error. There were incidents of missing money, but through the process of tracking it down, I would develop better and tighter ways of managing the cash going forward. There were a few larger cases of suspected embezzlement, but nothing crippling, and the theft was caught in time before significant damage could be done. There's always a paper trail to follow, even with cash, and it always leads to someone.

I brought in a forensic auditor a few times to take a deeper dive into following the paper trail, as I had neither the time nor skill set myself. Other times, I brought in my attorney. Sometimes employees were released; sometimes resignations were accepted. No charges were ever pressed. Every retailer deals with shrinkage, theft, and loss. It simply goes with the territory. I accepted that this was going to happen and chose to mitigate it by learning from mistakes, constantly improving policies and systems, and doing everything I could to hire trustworthy people.

On a daily basis, the cash management and cash processing were full-time jobs. Stop and think for a moment about the time it would take out of your day if you received all of your income in cash and likewise had to pay all of your bills the same way. You would have a lot less free time than you do now. After trying many different methods for reconciling the daily cash flow and each of them falling apart due to too many people being involved with the process, I finally hit on a system that worked. I held each store manager accountable for their store's cash at the end of each night. From there, I had a single individual whose primary responsibility was to check their work, "deposit" the money, and then reallocate it (based on internal formulas and budgeting) to the appropriate account payable. This seems simple, but with the type of revenue numbers the two stores were generating, it was a full-time job—more than that actually since eventually I had to find her an assistant to reduce all the overtime she was working. Reducing the number of people with fingers in the cash pie greatly reduced the margin of error, but it was also an enormous amount of trust to place in one person. At the end of the day, you have to be able to trust your people. I also had the utmost confidence that I could very quickly and easily run my own audits on her work to ensure every penny was accounted for and where it should be. This was a necessary part of the double-verification process, of verifying the verifiers. Although trust is critically important, accountability is even more so.

Aside from the overwhelming logistics of managing the cash, my other priority was security. The stores' revenue came from a single source—the cash registers. However, it went out in a lot of different directions, and each one of those directions had different security issues. Payments made to vendors had to be pulled from the safe and counted a second time by the person receiving them, acknowledging that the payments were accurate. We always got signatures, even before this was a state requirement.

The sales tax the stores collected was paid directly to a local branch of the California Department of Tax and Fee Administration in Redding. During preregulation, we could walk in a payment on any day of the week that suited us. From a security perspective, this was great because we could get the cash out of the store. In postregulation, the agency changed its policy and would only let us come in once a month and required a scheduled appointment since they had to coordinate with the California Highway Patrol for security during all drop-offs. During a peak month in 2020, the stores were generating combined sales tax revenue of just under $100,000. The two cities to whom we owed cannabis tax were more flexible and allowed weekly payments at our convenience. For that same peak month in 2020, the combined city taxes were around $60,000.

What most people don't realize is that even with that heavy volume, the cash went right back out as quickly as it came in. When you're a commodity-based operation locked onto a strong growth trajectory, as both stores were, the products need constant replenishment and always at a higher level than the previous month in order to support that growth. Similarly, the payroll budget keeps increasing as more employees are needed to accommodate the increased traffic that is responsible for the increased revenue. It is a never-ending cycle of earning and spending.

However, there were frightening times during that cycle when the cash would literally begin to pile up, either because it was right before a payday or tax-payment date, or because several vendors were late in coming to collect payment. I hated all those eggs sitting there in one basket, so I would diversify my assets. In this case, "diversification" meant grabbing my shoeboxes and withdrawing most of the cash from the safe (entering my withdrawals properly into the tracking software, of course), moving it offsite to an undisclosed location, and bringing it back just before it was to be spent on tax or distributor payments.

This was not safe, I realize, but neither was leaving hundreds of thousands of dollars sitting in one location, ripe for the picking. I went to great lengths to keep my personal addresses very private, and I made sure I drove a secure, reliable vehicle. And then there was Zeus, my protection K9 who didn't like anyone, including my staff (and to be fair, the feeling was mutual).

Although it was nice to see the beefed-up security in the CDTFA branch while watching them count out the payment, we still had to get it to them, just as we had to get it across town to the cities, and I still had to diversify the cash off-site. These were large amounts of money being transported on public roadways, and it was not safe. Armored transport was out of the question because, like banks and credit unions, they are also federally regulated and would not touch cannabis money.

I am beyond grateful that in eleven years, we never had a major security incident and that all my employees stayed safe. During that time, I had only three minor security incidents, one at 530 and two at Synergy. In each case, the law-enforcement response and support were tremendous. Every deputy I ever interacted with, all the way up to the chief, was professional, respectful, and supportive.

I could ask for nothing more.

Well, except maybe federal legalization.

THE TEAM

Team building is an art. It involves carefully and strategically weaving the dynamics and energy of individual personalities to create a balanced, cohesive tapestry that is seamless in its focus and mission, at least while on the clock. While I cannot claim to have mastered the art, I did learn some profound lessons, and developed viable strategies around team building.

Second only to the customers, the team is the most integral part of a retail operation—and maybe not even second, as the relationship between the customers and the team is truly symbiotic.

Perhaps one of the surprising aspects of team building that I came to realize over the years was that the team comprised not just individuals, but it was a living thing all its own, the same way that a marriage is its own force beyond the two individuals in the relationship. Looking out for the team and its overall health, as well as its individual members, required making decisions that maintained balance and equanimity. Sometimes those decisions meant passing on a sparkling candidate with a dream résumé because my instinct told me that their personality would never mesh with the existing team. I had learned that the inevitable drama that was bound to result from such personality conflicts would drastically outweigh the benefits of hiring that sparkling individual. It also sometimes meant that an individual best suited for the job was not promoted and a lesser-qualified individual was.

In this regard, team management is like a chess game. It involves strategic thinking, weighing alternatives, then executing moves based on the immediate dynamics of the game (the team) at hand.

I often found myself in an interview, explaining to a candidate why someone's past cannabis experience and knowledge were of little interest to me, much to the disappointment of the individual who clearly assumed their prior cannabis employment history made them a shoo-in for the job. Conversely, this information was received with optimistic surprise by the individual who thought they never had a shot at a job with my company because of their lack of cannabis experience. I explained to both that I could teach anyone all they needed to know about cannabis, in the scope of retail at least. That was just book-learning. What I couldn't teach but what was infinitely more valuable was their personality. More specifically, how they would blend with the existing team and how well they would mesh with the customers. Using this metric alone, I could often tell within a matter of minutes if a candidate was a yes or a no. I applied this same metric when evaluating internal candidates for a promotion.

Several times over the years, I found myself with a vacancy to fill. I always tried to promote from within whenever possible. In mentally reviewing my list of candidates, I often had to choose between a newer employee with the right skill set for the job and a more long-standing veteran who I knew wanted the job. In those instances, I had to weigh not only longevity and a solid-performance track record but also a lesser skill set against someone who was the best fit. More often than not,

I chose to promote the less skilled individual, though know-ing I'd have to spend more time on training and development, because that was the best decision for the balance of the team as a whole. To promote a newer—even if more skilled—staff member over a less skilled veteran would have meant poten-tial disgruntlement, resentment, and decreased performance, even potentially creating a security risk, that could have easily infected the team at large.

I had not realized when I opened 530 Collective in 2009 that owning and running a business was more about people management than anything else. Had my degree been in busi-ness, I probably would have known this from the outset, but as it was, I learned this point by living it, as I had done in so many other areas.

Somewhat to my surprise, employee management was one of the most rewarding aspects of business ownership. To watch an individual's personal and professional growth, to see them successfully challenge themselves, push their boundaries, and become a leader in their own right—and know that I had helped facilitate that growth—was incredibly gratifying.

One of the most beautiful examples of this was Monika Bent. "Mo" started with 530 Cannabis in 2015 as a kitchen assistant for the 530 Edibles line. Although very quiet, she demonstrated one of the strongest work ethics that I've ever seen. She showed up on time, did anything asked of her, and never brought any toxic drama, a quality that, as I learned, is both rare and valuable to any team.

But I also learned very quickly that she did not like helping the customers. Fortunately, her position in the kitchen didn't require direct customer interaction, but in a small retail envi-ronment, she was forced to interact with clients occasionally when restocking the display cases with edibles. She hated that part of her job.

When the time came to close the edibles kitchen and lay off my head chef, I felt certain that I would lose Mo as well, given that the only remaining positions were customer-facing. Consequently, I was shocked when she came to me, nervous as hell, and told me she really wanted to stay on with the company. She said she loved working in the cannabis industry; she loved the company and didn't want to leave. I still remember the fear in her eyes that I had already made the decision to let her go.

I was direct with her. I told her that any position I moved her into would involve customer interaction, and I knew that was something she did not enjoy.

She told me she that she could learn how to be nice to the customers.

My heart went out to her, and I was impressed by her surprising and bold request. I knew she was absolutely genuine.

I said, "OK, prove it."

And she did. Mo learned how to ask customers open-ended questions in order to help guide them toward the most appropriate products, and she gained confidence in using her extensive personal knowledge of the product to help them make the best selections for themselves. Surprisingly— perhaps to herself more than anyone—Mo was damn good with the customers.

There were a couple of other reasons why I kept her on. I had learned that she had been with Taco Bell for seven years prior to coming to my team. My very first real-world job at age fifteen and a half was with Jack in the Box. I stayed for one year. I knew exactly what fast-food work is like, and I was even more impressed by her tenacity to stay in that industry for as long as she had. That alone set her apart.

Additionally, I figured she knew what a shitty job was like and would, consequently, have much more appreciation for a good job. I've no doubt it was that appreciation that drove her to express her desire to stay.

The final reason I kept her on was because at that time, and still to this day, very few members of my teams have challenged me or surprised me. Mo did both.

She knew what she wanted; she had the confidence to support her position, and she found the courage to ask. In exchange for her courage and the competence that went with it, I gave her an opportunity.

When I opened my second store, Synergy, Mo told me she wanted to be part of the new team, so I promoted her to head security guard. She kept asking for more responsibility and kept showing me she deserved it. From security, I moved her onto the management team and eventually put her in charge of METRC, the touchpoint for every cannabis operator's inventory within the state's track and trace system.

To this day, I am still inspired by Mo's courage and willingness to always push herself to grow, to improve, and to be her best.

Sometimes keeping the team's equilibrium meant knowing when to overlook the policy breach of an otherwise superb employee because losing them would completely disrupt the entire operation.

Shelley Mason came to the 530 Cannabis team in the middle of 2017 after serving seventeen years in the medical industry as a practice manager and a medical assistant for a urology surgical group. Initially, I didn't have enough direct interaction with Shelley personally to evaluate her work performance, but time and time again her name would come up very positively in the weekly manager meetings. She began to show herself to the team, and by default to me, as thoughtful, thorough, proactive, and extraordinarily competent.

Consequently, when I began building out my team for the second store, in 2018, I knew I wanted Shelley on it, and I wanted her toward the top, directly reporting to me.

She moved to Synergy initially in an administrative role, but her tasks quickly grew into full accounts payable and receivable, human relations, and even budgeting. She was never in a formal management role, but she acquired some of those responsibilities as she became one to whom the staff turned for support and guidance.

During Synergy's rollout in 2018 and the exponential growth of that store, I turned to her as well, time and time again, to be my sounding board, even more often than I consulted those who were technically higher on the company organizational chart.

And yet during our last year together, I almost released her from employment.

The incident involved Shelley taking company files home so she could catch up on some work over the weekend. While well intended, this was a serious breach in company policy for several reasons, some of which had legal ramifications. For Shelley, the lapse in judgment could not have been more poorly timed.

When the incident with Shelley struck, I had just spent months trying to repair another employee debacle with a long-term manager. Ultimately, my attempts had failed, and I'd had to accept their resignation. So, when Shelley's blunder occurred, I found myself jaded, fed up, and simply out of patience with regard to employee infractions.

I was in no mood for second chances and had almost made up my mind to let her go over the single policy violation.

Fortunately for both of us, I slept on it. I had learned that with any decision I found myself conflicted over or that would have a profound impact on the business, a solid night's sleep before that final decision had always proved to be a good idea.

In the optimism that always comes with each new day, I made the decision to evaluate Shelley based on her overall performance and devotion to the companies rather than to focus on the one incident of poor judgment and dismiss her past positive contributions. I kept her on and in doing so, made one of my best decisions to date. I trusted my gut; she was simply too good to lose.

That last year that we were together, and particularly the last several months up to the High Times acquisition, she became both my right- and left-hand woman. I am not joking when I say that I knew the teams could get by without me, but to try getting by without Shelley would have been devastating.

The strategic thought process that is required in employee management, as well as other areas of the business, was something that served me well in building a strong team and recognizing potential in certain individuals who initially needed some polishing or nurturing and development to reach that potential. Once developed, they became invaluable members of the organization, often in roles unrelated to or far more advanced than their initial position. One individual in particular comes to mind in this respect.

Colby Law was in the first round of interviews I conducted for the Synergy store in the summer of 2018, and I almost didn't hire him.

The interviews that day were for the consultant position, my revamped term for budtender. Since that position spent nearly every moment of their shift directly engaged with the customer, I was looking for individuals who were outgoing, enthusiastic, and dynamic. While I did not see those traits in Colby and, consequently, did not think him suited for the consultant position, I did notice that he had a calm confidence about him that I liked.

It was because of that calm confidence, combined with my buyer's stamp of approval, that I offered him a position in security.

In the security role, Colby thrived. He demonstrated an impeccable work ethic combined with an uncommonly positive attitude. He showed up motivated and in a good mood every day. Not the bubbly, cheerleader type of good mood—plenty of other staff filled that role—but just genuine positivity. This quality, combined with an unparalleled work ethic and unshakable poise even when dealing with the most difficult customers, eventually earned him a place on the management team.

Several months into his new leadership position, Colby started to bring me ideas. But, more important, it was the thought process behind his ideas that really got my attention.

It was not particularly unusual for my managers to bring me ideas. I had developed a routine of holding regular roundtable meetings with my management teams, sometimes weekly if needed, but at least twice a month. These roundtables were a time for check-ins, discussions about employee relations, conversations about company policy changes, brainstorming, and even the occasional bitch session.

What I fostered in my team was the confidence to bring forth ideas to improve the company as a whole, and I provided a safe environment in which to do it. I told them repeatedly that I was only one set of eyes and one brain and that I needed all of theirs to help further the growth of the company. They knew I was always looking to improve, always striving to do something better tomorrow than we did yesterday. I told the team that even though I had a lot of ideas myself, they were not all good ideas, and that I wanted their thoughts on how we could improve. If their idea seemed solid, we would roll it out.

So, the fact that Colby was bringing me an idea was not what set him apart. Instead, it was the fact that his ideas were strategic and logistic; he was thinking outside the box, pre-empting potential problems and coming up with his own solutions, all without anyone asking him to do so. That was just how his mind worked, and I couldn't believe I was just now discovering it.

In hiring interviews, he was able to read between the lines of what the interviewee was saying and drill down to potential impacts to the company; he was able to project possible impacts to the operations as a result of COVID and find viable work-arounds; he was able to see data-driven ways to streamline our delivery service to maximize efficiency.

In short, he was thinking about the business the same way that I thought about it. And he did all of this without my ever asking.

It had taken me almost two years to discover this about Colby, but I started immediately looking for more ways in which I could cultivate his talent, even coaching him directly in ways that would enhance what already came naturally to him, and in particular, how it pertained to company operations and management as a whole.

I also immediately moved him from his floor-management position into a position within the buying team, which was struggling at the time. It was my hope that Colby would bring his strategic-thinking and problem-solving skills to bear on the buying department.

I never would have thought that the quiet individual whom I almost passed over would prove himself to be such a competent and rare asset to the team.

As much care as I took to build the team strategically and hire individuals who I hoped would mesh and balance with the existing team and help move the companies forward in a positive way, I will be the first to admit that I failed as often as I succeeded in that area. While some of the individuals who ended up being the greatest assets to the team were the ones I never expected to excel, many of those whom I hired because of their rock star résumé never lived up to expectations. Some individuals simply know how to interview well, to say all the right things to get the job, but then once they have the job, it becomes clear that they really have no interest in the work. Human nature and psychology are funny like that.

The harsh reality is that employee management can be downright devastating, both personally and professionally.

This was particularly true in one instance with a long-tenured employee whom I had promoted several times—and whom, against every rule of business ownership, I had also considered a friend—but seemingly out of nowhere began failing in his duties. After months of attempting to rehabilitate him, I was forced to accept his resignation. He had been with the company for six years, and I was bitterly disappointed and deeply saddened by his departure.

In another instance, I discovered that a relatively new employee had an aptitude for financials and immediately shifted them to an appropriate position. Several months later, I learned that the financials were in terrible disarray—likely intentionally to distract from the significant variances. This individual had covered their tracks well initially, but the paper trail had caught up to them. Upon further investigation, I discovered that money was missing. In this case the anger I felt over the alleged betrayal outweighed any disappointment over their departure, and I happily accepted their resignation.

Inevitably there were times I would have to terminate an individual's employment. This was never something I took lightly, and this was perhaps the hardest part of my job as a business owner. Unless I was out of town and the situation required immediate attention, I always administered employee terminations myself. I felt that I owed them the respect of delivering that message myself.

The most unexpected and conflicted of these situations took place in January 2019. I was not on-site for the incident, but I was later able to review security camera footage.

A verbal altercation had taken place in the dispensing room at 530 Cannabis between one of the store's regular customers and a budtender. A hate-based slur directed toward the budtender made its way into the dialogue. At this point, a manager got involved and proceeded to escort the customer out of the building, which was absolutely the right thing to do and in line with their managerial job duties; hate-based anything was never tolerated in any of my establishments.

The customer left but stood in the parking lot still engaged in conversation with the manager, who was standing in the open doorway. The customer then said something that escalated the tension further. The manager turned back into the store, picked up a lobby chair, and returned to the doorway, brandishing the chair over their head, advancing on the customer. Fortunately, other team members intercepted them and returned both chair and manager into the building.

In principle, I applauded the passion with which the manager stood up for their coworker and stood against hate-based speech, something the company had a staunch and long-standing policy against. However, any employee brandishing anything—excepting possibly colorful language—against any other individual could have only one possible ending. I released that manager from employment, making sure to have a security guard in the room when I did so. The customer I banned from shopping in the store indefinitely. Never a dull moment in the life of an entrepreneur!

With team members like Mo, Colby, and Shelley, I learned to look beyond the résumé, sometimes beyond the initial impression, to discover the talent that was beneath, waiting to be given the opportunity to shine. I was always thrilled to discover diamonds in the rough. They are the ones that make team building worthwhile.

Over the years, I've received numerous compliments on what I have built and what I have achieved. Some of the praise has been directed at the stores, some given to me personally. The compliments often include words like "professional," "knowledgeable," and "pioneering." Sometimes the source of these accolades tells me how proud I should be of all I've done and all I've accomplished. I receive the praise politely but always with an awkward feeling because those compliments really don't belong to me. They belong to the team, as I politely tell whoever is standing in front of me.

I tell them that while I may have the vision, it is the *team* that brings that vision to life. I tell them that I could not have done anything without my team. I can't mean that fiercely enough.

GREED

Given that I had two incredibly successful stores and a rock-solid track record of government and community outreach, many may wonder why I decided to sell. In answering that question, I will repeat something I said at the very beginning of this book, and I think this time most will believe me: it wasn't about the money.

In growing my operations from one store to two, from a single cash register to a combined thirteen, from revenue of less than $100,000 to nearly $12 million, from seeing 530 Cannabis awarded two of the first ten Bureau of Cannabis Control licenses in the state, to seeing Synergy awarded the first state retail license in Redding, I had poured blood, sweat, and literally tears into these two stores, pursuing my ever-arching goal to be the best: to be the best retailer in the north state; to provide the best retail experience to the customer; to be the best employer for my staff.

To keep in line with those goals, for my stores to remain market leaders and maintain relevance for another eleven years, to ensure the individuals on my teams could continue to flourish professionally with even more opportunities before them than I could ever hope to offer, meant turning them over to someone who could not only maintain what I had built but do so at the next level.

There is a changing of the guard taking place in this industry, and it was time for me to gracefully bow out and hand my businesses over to the next generation of operator. There was no shortage of big players and well-moneyed interests looking to get into the cannabis industry. I was contacted by a few local individuals and groups as well as several from other parts of California. My stores had even drawn interest from groups across the country. But I was looking for the best for my stores and my team.

I went through a few different mergers and acquisitions (M&A) consultants before I found the incredibly talented gentlemen of Hunt Equity, the ones to get the acquisition across the finish line in the summer of 2020, in the middle of a pandemic with the absolute best possible buyer imaginable to successfully tackle "Cannabis 2.0." I wanted nothing less for my team.

I am proud and humbled to be fortunate enough to leave my businesses, and my team, in the very capable hands of the iconic brand High Times.

A few weeks before the acquisition was finalized, my staff gave me a surprise going-away party. The instigator was Jacqueline Garcia, the one and only friend whom I hired into my businesses and only then because she and I had reached an understanding that even if it turned out she hated working for me or if I had to fire her, we would still remain friends. Fortunately, neither of those things happened. So, when Jacquie texted me that she wanted to get together for a drink before the acquisition closed, I had no reason to suspect it was going to be anything more than that.

Walking into the elegant dining room at View 202 and seeing nearly every staff member waving and smiling at me, the table already laid with mouthwatering appetizers and my favorite bottle of red wine, was absolutely brilliant, and it was indeed a fabulous surprise.

Toward the end of the party, the team gathered naturally and said some words in tribute to their experience working with me. I have always been uncomfortable receiving compliments or praise. I'm not sure why. (I'm sure Dr. Z. has some ideas.)

So I stood there and received their compliments and praise, feeling awkward and uncomfortable, a little bit proud and a lot humbled. And very deeply moved. There emerged a recurring theme to many of the compliments: a theme of generosity, how unlike their former employers I was in that regard. Then one of them said one of the things he admired most about me was that I'm not greedy. I saw many heads nod and heard many murmurs of agreement.

But they are wrong. I am most definitely greedy. Perhaps not in the way they meant, but greedy nonetheless.

I am greedy for life, greedy for its experiences: the warm reciprocity of family and friendship, the pleasure of improving others' quality of life, the passion of a loving relationship, the exhilaration of exercise and health, the adventure of exploring other cultures, the joy of caring for my menagerie of critters, the achievement of growing a successful business, the satisfaction of a job well done. I am greedy for all of those things. Above all, however, I am greedy to make things better. And yes, by default, a facet of "experiences" must involve the experience of financial success, of prosperity.

While the experiences may be the end result, the motivation, the driving force toward that endgame, is equally important, if not more so. For me, the starting point, the motivator, was always pursuing my dream of owning my own business, and as that path opened up and I began to walk it, that dream and its motivators began to evolve into my desire to make a difference, to make things better, and to be the best. My initial vision contained elements of these next-generation motivators: to create a store that was different from the options available in 2009, different in its inclusivity rather than exclusivity. This rough sketch I would eventually evolve into a more concrete definition of what being "the best" means: to provide the best retail experience for the customer, to be the best employer, and to be the best individual that I could possibly be. As those elements manifested in the company's increased growth and subsequently increased revenue stream, I realized there was a direct correlation between the store's financial success and my ability to make things better for those around me.

Be it right or wrong, financial success is the most common bar by which we define overall success in American society.

So, while my initial motivation to roll the dice in this small business venture was not money, I found that money was increasingly becoming a focal point of external sources; I was realizing that as the company grew, so did the target on my back.

As my first store, 530 Collective, became more successful—meaning at first that it didn't go under and the doors continued to stay open—cannabis remained a hot topic in the community. The media is always interested in any controversial issue. I found my phone ringing often with requests for interviews, and I never turned them down. Anytime a reporter wanted to talk, I made time for a conversation. This media presence, coupled with my willingness and, in fact, intention, to collaborate with city officials and law enforcement, drew some fire. There have always been plenty of industry advocates and operators who felt cannabis and cops couldn't be on the same side, and I represented another perspective. But the sharpest criticism was, surprisingly, around money.

None of my critics' voices were terribly loud, but they were persistent. I have always expected that with success comes criticism, and that has never daunted me. What I found interesting were the source and the subject of the criticism.

I was accused, tried, and convicted of being greedy.

Surprisingly, there were individuals within my own industry, even some of my own customers, who were critical of my financial success. As my critics saw the traffic in the store increase, more product offerings, and bigger staff, they voiced negativity. I was surprised by the snide remarks I heard about how much money the store must be making if I could afford to hire all these people. I heard comments about how it must be nice to afford a new car (which happened to be a used Volvo station wagon). I fielded complaints that the store wasn't giving away enough free product to customers when it could obviously afford to. I was utterly confused.

Some of the local advocates and even some of the customers held the belief that I should, obviously, be successful enough to be there for them, to provide cannabis on a daily basis, or be there to further the intent of the industry at large, but clearly in their eyes, I wasn't supposed to be too successful. What is that even supposed to mean, *too successful*?

The bottom line was they felt that I was making too much money.

But too much by whose standard? Would some of those critics have been appeased if I had kept struggling to make my personal ends meet, as was the case in the early months and even years of the store? Would they have been pleased to know that John and I had lost our home to foreclosure in order to keep the store? Would they have found it acceptable if my annual salary were always lower than theirs? Who was setting this bar?

I was experiencing the effects of both success shaming and the tallest-poppy syndrome, that strange phenomenon that exists in society whereby some strive to cut off the heads of others in order to make themselves feel taller.

As 530 Cannabis, and later Synergy, became more and more financially successful, that success meant I could hire more people. I could give raises and bonuses to my existing staff. I could offer more vacation hours to the team. I could contribute significantly to local community benefit programs. I could host and donate to community events. I could help an employee buy a car when theirs broke down completely. I could bring more products to the shelves for the customers. I could make physical improvements to the facilities to enhance the customer experience. I could buy my teams lunch on a regular basis. I could bring in a massage therapist every month so the staff could really relax on their breaks, and I could throw the team one hell of a Christmas party.

The higher the gross revenue numbers climbed, the more tax revenue was generated for the two cities, meaning those cities could fill law-enforcement vacancies, disburse building improvement grants, and make infrastructure improvements.

The increasing financial success of the stores was a win all around, from any angle; it was the rising tide that lifted many boats.

When all is said and done, I make no bones about being greedy, about wanting all the experiences that go with bringing my vision to life and seeing it flourish and thrive. It is those experiences that I find exhilarating. To me, they are the very heart and soul of success.

Drawing inspiration from Thoreau, I want all the experiences that go with sucking the marrow out of life and "not, when I come to die, discover that I have not lived."

Whether it's critics trumpeting accusations of greed, vindictive former employees fabricating claims in court, malicious and preposterous online chatter, or some other distraction, know that there will always be challenges in pursuing your vision and your dream. However, it will be up to you to decide if they are insurmountable or not.

To paraphrase the visionary Henry Ford, whether you think you can or you think you can't, either way you're right.

There will always be people trying to take you down one way or another. It's your job to tune out the noise and nay-sayers and stay the course. I chose to see every challenge and every obstacle as an opportunity. I chose to always find a solution. I chose to either win or learn.

I maintained this outlook by always returning to my vision. I reminded myself of my belief in it and my belief in myself. To those two things, I held true. Always.

When the dark days come, and they will, when self-doubt sneaks in at 3:00 a.m. and keeps you awake until dawn, when the only voices you seem to hear are those of your critics, then grab your headphones, find your source of joy, and focus your lens back on your vision.

My cannabis journey from 2009 through 2020 was a roller coaster of experiences unlike any other: seeing the industry evolve from the Wild West of cannabis to full legalization; advocating both locally and in the state capitol for the policy as well as the process; witnessing the individual members of my team grow and thrive both personally and professionally; seeing with exhilaration all of our hard work pay off; and above all, learning, challenging, and growing myself.

Every.

Single.

Day.

I've always taken mischievous pleasure in doing things my own way, and it was a combination of that propensity toward unconventionality, deep-rooted tenacity, and an absolutely rock-solid team that became the strongest drivers behind the stores' success.

This has been the hardest "job" I have ever had and undoubtedly the most rewarding.

I would do it all again in a heartbeat, and I wouldn't trade the experience for anything.

As to what is next for me, I defer to the timeless David Bowie: "I don't know where I'm going from here, but I promise it won't be boring."

EPILOGUE

As one story ends and another story emerges, it is not surprising that I find myself composing these words, walking along the beach as I have done so many times before. The tranquility of the ocean this day incites one of the most vibrant memories I have from early childhood—Doran Beach in Sonoma County, the snapshot etched in my mind full of comforting sunshine, sandcastles, playful waves, and my mom.

Whether because that profound yet fleeting childhood memory is full of uncomplicated happiness or because the ocean touches my soul, I have found myself returning, again and again, to its solace and its energy throughout my life.

There is nothing terribly unique in the fact that I draw inspiration from the ocean. That it calls to many of us is a fact proven by the price of coastal real estate the world over and supported in evidence by the millions who, year in and year out, make beaches on every continent their vacation destination.

But what is it about the ocean that draws us? Is it that the ocean is a living, breathing entity both biologically as well as spiritually? Is it because it harkens back to our earliest days in the womb? Or is it simply its undeniable beauty? Whatever the reason, the ocean's vigorous assault on each of our five primary senses cannot be ignored: we taste the tang of the salt on our palate; we inhale the aroma of kelp; we feel the foam dance around our ankles; and we see the sparkle of the sunlight off the waves—no two glimmers ever alike—and we hear the voice of the surf in all of its moods.

Yet for me, there is a sixth sense with which the ocean resonates: it touches my soul; it is a source of pure, unadulterated joy.

While it has been years since I've paddled out, I taught myself how to surf when I moved to San Diego in my early twenties. There is nothing on earth like the feeling of being out in the ocean, sitting on your board watching the sets come in, and finally catching that wave. During that time in San Diego, I managed to get out in the water almost daily, sometimes twice a day if the surf was particularly fun. I always looked for the least crowded breaks even if it meant I would compromise the quality of surf. I enjoyed the tranquility of surfing alone.

There, surfing alone, I would find myself both energized and yet at peace.

Even if not immersed in it physically, being close enough to the ocean to see it, hear it, smell it still has that exhilarating effect on my inner being. It is a source of both inspiration and joy; it is to the ocean that I go to find myself.

I've talked throughout this book about my vision, about the importance of holding to it, of the necessity of believing in it. And the birth of any vision really begins with finding your joy.

Living as I did in Shasta County for fifteen years, over three hours from the nearest ocean, I had to find other sources of inspiration, other ways to connect with my source energy and to stay grounded. Sometimes it was the mountains, with which Shasta County abounds. Pine trees have also been my lifelong friends, and they are not without their own majestic, inspirational energy.

I will settle for a lake if that is my only other option. But never a river. Rivers are skulking and suspect.

In finding our joy, we create space—perhaps physical space but most definitely mental and emotional space—in which we can feel grounded, relaxed, and inspired; space in which we will do our best work in focusing on and honing our vision.

Virginia Woolf wrote that to be successful as a writer, a woman must have a room of her own, meaning both literal space without domestic demands but also space for women in general to have their space within the male-dominated literary world of her time.

Taking Virginia Woolf's words in a greater context, this sentiment holds true for everyone. Every individual needs their own space—a literal or figurative room of their own—in which to connect with their joy and in which to develop and grow their vision.

What I now tell people seeking my business advice is this: Whatever your vision, think of it as having its own life force. And what your vision needs to survive, more than anything, is space; you must give it room to breathe and grow if it is to thrive and evolve. My vision started with an idea for an enhanced experience within a single store, yet evolved into a mission to shatter stereotypes, legitimize an industry, and to always be the best. My vision was in constant evolution because it was and is alive, and yours will do the same. It will grow and expand as you nurture it. That evolution and expansion are part of the point.

It can be difficult—even seem impossible—to find the time, space, or energy to devote to your vision. The realities of life can easily get in the way; the demands of a job, children, a spouse; the distraction of social media and the online vortex;

the barrage of news and information we find ourselves subjected to from nearly every angle can be deafening, drowning out the softer voice of your vision sitting quietly in its corner of your heart and waiting patiently for you to bring it to life.

On a daily basis, I find joy in many things, not just actualizing my outer work in the world. I find joy in my dogs—three of them at the moment. Each one whimsically different from the other, yet each pure joy to me (excepting those times when they sneak my slippers from the closet and blissfully rip them to shreds—finding their own joy, no doubt). Jim finds his joy on the golf course; for my sister, Amy, the source of joy is the desert. Living as I do now, back near the beach, I am grateful to be able to reconnect with the ocean. Although I love the pines and the lakes, my first choice for joy, inspiration, and renewal is always the ocean.

Of course, I'm not blind to the feminine symbolism of the ocean. Perhaps my subconscious was always driving me there, showing me the joy within, all the while leading me down the path of rediscovering my vulnerability to culminate at a place I feel safe, a place to which I have returned time and again, a place where my soul feels energized and alive—the ocean.

Wherever or whatever your joy may be, I hope you find it. I hope you find that room of your own in which to carve out space and time to refocus and reenergize yourself and to let your vision thrive.

I hope you do this for the sake of your vision and for the life that you wish for, long for, and are meant for.

AFTERWORD

Embracing and regulating a complicated industry that had never been part of any government systems or oversight has been a Herculean challenge. We knew it would be difficult. Building systems from the ground up hasn't been easy. And a big part of the problem is that people in state and local government didn't know what they didn't know. Just understanding the complexities of cultivation and manufacturing, in particular, has taken significant time.

In the six years since the California legislature passed the Medical Cannabis Regulation and Safety Act and the voters approved Proposition 64, legalizing cannabis for adult use, a lot has happened, but quite frankly, a lot hasn't changed.

In 2015, my colleagues and I envisioned simple processes to encourage the industry to come out of the shadows and become a part of a regulated industry that would have significant benefits to everyone. Everything has proven far more complicated than we intended, and consequently, entrance into the regulated legal market has been much slower than expected. There is a thriving, and in some places growing, black market, which is the exact opposite of what we hoped might happen. For those who have embraced the process and managed to navigate the multiple agencies involved in licensing, I offer a big thank-you and congratulations. For those still trying to navigate what probably seems like an endless series of challenges, I ask you to please stick with it; we need you to be successful.

I fully expect that the process moving toward a market with more licensed businesses than not will take ten years.

What hasn't changed is the destruction of wildlife habitats and sensitive watersheds by unlicensed grows. This is the reason I waded into the cannabis issue. In some areas, it's actually worse. In the face of a historic drought, I cringe, knowing that illegal water diversions will only intensify the pressures on the environment. The wanton use of banned pesticides, poaching of game, polluting waterways, and the trashing of public and private land simply aren't going away. I truly thought that a pathway toward a legal, regulated market would begin to change those practices, but so far it really hasn't. There are literally thousands of abandoned grow sites that need to be cleaned up. I keep fighting for resources to do that, and I simply won't quit.

Clear signals from the federal government around banking and a truly hands-off approach to states with full legalization are vital to the success of these efforts. Full-scale legalization at the federal level feels years away, but with each state that opens to cannabis, the pressure to act and the momentum for change increases. There's even a growing "Congressional Cannabis Caucus" in the US House of Representatives. This is a positive sign that as more states legalize cannabis, there will be increased opportunities for substantive conversations at the federal level.

A bright spot in the regulatory process in many communities has been the retail cannabis businesses. Perhaps because of their visibility, they have brought clear benefits and resources to communities that have welcomed them. Here I have a personal bias with regard to Jamie. I watched her embrace the regulatory process and engage in it with gusto and enthusiasm. I watched as she anticipated changes and worked to be ahead of the curve. Her knowledge of regulations and statutes is almost encyclopedic. Frankly, I marveled at her success in engaging law enforcement, city councils, county supervisors, and the media. Her businesses were always open doors to anyone who wanted to learn and understand the industry. She was extremely professional and respectful of people with differing opinions about her business or cannabis in general. I honestly believe that is a winning strategy at all levels of the industry. People often fear what they don't understand, and it's very easy to fall back on timeworn stereotypes when they lack exposure to what's really going on in the world. It's a little like grassroots (pun intended) politics where you win hearts and minds one person at a time. Jamie mastered that, and her businesses thrived in one of the most conservative parts of California.

It's easy to glamorize being a business owner, but entrepreneurship is so much more difficult than people imagine. Twenty-four hours a day and seven days a week you are responsible for the business, your staff, and your customers. I knew it from twenty-seven years of practicing dentistry, and that understanding of what she was going through was a big part of our relationship when she owned the stores. There were times I offered support as her sounding board on some basic business issues but was honestly absolutely clueless on others.

I couldn't be prouder of Jamie. She's incredibly honest, unbelievably hardworking, fearless, and was extremely generous to her staff and her customers. She has instincts that rarely steered her astray and a vision that she uses as her guide.

As she moves through the adventure that is her life, a couple of certainties guide her: her everyday life will always be somewhat unconventional, and she will never settle for anything short of extraordinary.

Jim Wood
California State Assemblymember, District 2

ACKNOWLEDGMENTS

There was never a question of who would top my list of acknowledgments for this book: the customers. To each and every one of you who shopped in one of the stores, even if it was just once, thank you. And to those loyal customers who were with me from the very humble beginning, you have my deepest gratitude.

Secondly, I need to recognize the 530 and Synergy teams and every individual (regardless of how our working relationship may have ended) who was at one point part of the companies over the years. Each of you had a role in the overall success of the stores, and I thank you for being part of this journey and for believing in my vision to whatever extent you did.

And to Stephanie Pierce, for although she is mentioned in the book, its flow did not lend itself to really share my depth of appreciation of Stephanie. She was there through all of the darkest days, and throughout our ups and downs and her own personal battles, Stephanie never wavered in her loyalty to me or the companies. Stephanie, you are an angel on earth.

I am especially grateful to the City of Shasta Lake and the City of Redding for the honor and privilege of being part of their business communities. Thank you to all the city and law-enforcement officials who kept open minds when passing through my doors (I know my small brain has inadvertently left many names off this list, and for that I hope you will forgive me):

City of Shasta Lake: John Duckett, city manager; Jessica Lugo, assistant city manager; Steve Ayers, planning; Captain Forrest Bartell (Shasta County Sheriff's Office); Lieutenant Tom Campbell (SCSO); Sergeant Caleb McGregor (SCSO); Sergeant Tyler Thompson (SCSO); Sergeant Logan Stonehouse (SCSO); Sergeant John Greene (SCSO); the members of the city council and other appointed officials from 2009 through 2020.

City of Redding: Barry Tippin, city manager; Barry DeWalt, city attorney; Larry Vaupel, director of development services; Chief Roger Moore (Redding Police Department); Lieutenant Jeff Wallace (RPD); Officer Kurtis Stenderup (RPD); Officer Vega (RPD); the members of the city council and appointed officials from 2018 through 2020.

To Chris Hunt and Andrew Lampert, the brilliant and relentless duo at Hunt Equity, who worked tirelessly on the acquisition of my stores: Thank you for seeing it done! You guys are the best.

I am appreciative of every billable minute charged by my attorneys as their contribution to keeping me and my businesses in line. In order of acquaintance: Keith Cope, Ben Kennedy, Todd Endres, Stephen Osborne, Chris Dayans, Rich McDerby, and Nancy Nan.

Thank you to the executive team at High Times (Adam Levin, executive chairman; Peter Horvath, chief executive officer; Paul Henderson, president) for seeing value in what I built and folding my stores—and my teams—into the globally recognized High Times brand.

My publishing experience has been as incredible as everything else, and, in large part, that is because of the absolutely phenomenal Girl Friday Productions team and their commitment to professionalism, detail, and quality.

I owe a huge thank-you to the women at GFP who believed in my work and made it stronger. In the order of acquaintance: Christina Henry De Tessan, curator and development; Ingrid

Emerick, publisher; Katherine Richards, editor; Bethany Davis, editorial production; Georgie Hockett, marketing; Jane, copy-editor; Phyllis, proofreader.

A special thanks goes out to Gail Hudson, my developmental editor, for her valuable insight on the manuscript and for always looking out for my reader.

To my family and dear friends—specifically Rob Etulain, Amy Garzot, Rory Garzot, Judy Garzot, Dr. Z., Lori Ajax, and Jim Wood—who read early drafts of the manuscript, suffering through innumerable typos and entertaining dictation errors, thank you for taking the time to provide real and honest feedback that was incredibly valuable. I appreciate your support beyond words.

And finally, an additional thank-you to Jim for pushing me to not only do this but to do it *now*, while everything was fresh in my mind. Thank you for your unwavering confidence in me, in this project, and in "all of the things."

ABOUT THE AUTHOR

With eleven years of lawful cannabis industry experience, Jamie Andrea Garzot is one of California's pioneers, drawing from boots-on-the-ground experience as a state-licensed cannabis retailer, an appointed city official, and an industry advocate.

Since the beginning of her industry tenure in 2009, Garzot has logged thousands of hours advocating for responsible cannabis regulation before the California State Legislature and provided cannabis policy guidance to local governments throughout the Northern California region.

In August 2020, both of her groundbreaking businesses—530 Cannabis and Synergy—were acquired by the most globally recognized name in cannabis, High Times.

Jamie holds a Bachelor of Arts degree in English from San Diego State University, with her emphasis in British literature.

Jamie remains a high-profile industry advocate, educator, and public speaker.

She shares her life with her partner, Jim Wood, and their growing menagerie.